UNLESS SOME MAN SHOW ME

P. B. Fitzgerald

Bray

1962.

ALEXANDER JONES

S.T.L., L.S.S.

UNLESS SOME MAN SHOW ME

SHEED AND WARD

LONDON AND NEW YORK

FIRST PUBLISHED 1951
SHEED AND WARD, LTD.
33 MAIDEN LANE
LONDON W.C.2
AND
SHEED AND WARD, INC.
64 UNIVERSITY PLACE
NEW YORK, 3
FIRST STAGBOOK EDITION 1961

NIHIL OBSTAT: JOSEPH CARTNELL, S.T.D. CENSOR LIB.
IMPRIMATUR: DIE 30 SEPTEMBRIS 1950
✠ RICHARDUS, ARCHIEPISCOPUS LIVERPOLITANUS

PRINTED IN GREAT BRITAIN
BY LOWE AND BRYDONE (PRINTERS) LIMITED
LONDON, N.W.10

MATRI IMPRIMIS COELESTI
MEMORIAE DEIN TERRESTRIS
SORORI CARISSIMAE GRATO ANIMO

FOREWORD

THESE pages are written for the average person. Few have time or taste for the rich food of biblical learning as it is presented in weighty volumes and yet we all need the nourishment. This is an attempt to offer a little of it in light form for delicate digestions. The style is therefore a shade unconventional. I hope it will not be thought facetious and flippant, or rather that nobody will infer that one thinks lightly upon these grave matters. The first might be excused, being an error of policy; the second would be intolerable as an offence against piety. Where the honour of the Word of God and the dignity of Catholic exegesis are concerned there may be room for simple style but not for superficial thought.

A glance at the page of contents will show the purpose of this little collection. It is briefly this: to state and to stress certain particularly useful principles of interpretation within the traditional Catholic doctrine of Inspiration and Inerrancy and to apply these principles to one or two knotty questions of the Old Testament. This should help to show those who reverence the Old Testament as the Word of God how to protect it from ill-informed ridicule. The last four essays, and especially the last two, are written with an eye to our Jewish friends, the "kinsmen" whom St. Paul mourned and for whom God waits.

All of the articles have appeared in the *Catholic Gazette* (1948–1950) which is the monthly of the Catholic Missionary Society. I doubt if they would have appeared in book-form were it not for the many kind letters of readers who suggested it. I would thank most warmly an old friend, Fr. George Dwyer D.D., editor of the *Gazette*, both for his encouragement and for his acute and witty strictures. Certain of the qualities of this little book are due to him, none of its defects.

It is needless to say that the author is no official mouth-piece of the Catholic Church but a loyal son willing to interpret her mind and justify her ways. To her care and to her judgment he commits himself without reserve.

Upholland College
May 7, 1950

And behold, a man of Ethiopia, an eunuch, of great authority under Candace the queen of the Ethiopians, who had charge over all her treasures, had come to Jerusalem to adore.

And he was returning, sitting in his chariot and reading Isaias the prophet.

And the Spirit said to Philip: Go near and join thyself to this chariot.

And Philip running thither, heard him reading the prophet Isaias. And he said: Thinkest thou that thou understandest what thou readest?

Who said: And how can I, unless some man shew me?

Acts viii. 27–31

CONTENTS

THE PARADOX OF THE OLD TESTAMENT

ADAM'S APPLE has stuck in many a throat and wits have observed that it needs a pillar of salt to digest the "Whale" story. It is indeed in such simple and concrete fashion that the human mind loves to sum up its difficulties. But if gibe there must be, at least let the gibe be accurate. This matter of the "apple", for instance, should be scanned. It is not of importance for its own sake—"apple" or simply "fruit" makes no difference to the problem of interpretation—but, by some psychological twist, it is popularly supposed that the mention of a specific fruit demonstrates more effectively the absurdity of the "Fall" story. Now it is not Genesis that speaks of the apple, you know. The Hebrew word can mean anything from a vegetable to a vine. Why not a fig, for example? After all, this is the only fruit mentioned by name in the "Fall" narrative (Gen. iii. 7). Then where did the "apple" idea come from? First thoughts would suppose it five hundred years old in England:

> And al was for an appil,
>   an appil that he tok
> As clerkes fyndyn
>   wretyn in here book.

Second thoughts suggest that the word "appil", like its Latin brother, was "used from the earliest period with the greatest latitude" (I quote the *Oxford Dictionary*). Whatever the date of its birth, the idea probably originated from

a false interpretation of a faulty translation of the Canticle
of Canticles (viii. 5). The right translation is:

> *Under the apple-tree I awakened thee,*
> *in the house where thy mother gave thee birth.*

But the Vulgate (followed by Douay) reads:

> *Under the apple-tree I raised thee up,*
> *there thy mother was corrupted.*

In the former, correct, version the "apple-tree" is a
metaphor for the bridegroom under whose "shade" and
protection the bride delights (as in Cant. ii. 3); he therefore wakens her in his arms. The Vulgate, on the other
hand, appears to have taken the "apple-tree" quite
literally and this, *plus* the reading "corruption" took its
thoughts to the fall of mother Eve. Thenceforward Eve
and the "apple" were fated to appear together. As for the
"whale" we mentioned ("great fish" in the book of
Jonas), I doubt if the landlubber Hebrews knew the
animal.

Yet I fear that the reader of these essays who is licking his
lips in anticipation of a banquet of apples and whales
must straightway unlick them to go either grimly on or
empty away. For these are not the real problems of the
Old Testament. If we were to answer them we should be
little nearer to the meaning and purpose of the Old
Testament as a whole. The real problem is graver far and
its solution correspondingly more profound and more
instructive. Oh, there is more in the Old Testament than
the apples and whales and jawbones that fill the heckler's
handcart. Is it not the way of mental childhood to fasten
on the picturesque? To judge the substance by the appearance? A very small friend of mine once declared his peach

and cream the nicest fried egg he had ever tasted. Let us not be children in this weighty matter. Even a child, for instance, could notice that there are as many murders in Shakespeare's *Hamlet* as there are in Agatha Christie's *Ten Little Niggers*, but I feel sure that Miss Christie herself would be prepared to admit that this does not exhaust the comparison.

The real problem is this: that the Old Testament is dead and yet it lives. "You are dead to the Law", says St. Paul, announcing the new life in Christ (Rom. vii. 4). He was no more than interpreting the broad hint given by our Lord himself in the Sermon on the Mount: "It was said to them of old . . . but *I* say to you. . . ." (Matt. v. 21ff.). What does this mean? Surely the Old Testament was the "word of God"? Can the word of God die, then? It would seem so. And yet, by the command of God through the Church, the Old Testament is still commended to our attention side by side with the New; by God's command it still lives. And, truly, "not one jot or tittle of the Law shall pass", says our Lord. St. Paul is equally insistent: "Do we then destroy the Law through faith? God forbid! But we establish the Law" (Matt v. 18; Rom. iii. 31). A pretty problem! A dead thing that lives; a word of God that passes and does not pass. Refuse this Old Testament life, refuse it death—in either case the paradox dissolves. But we can do neither because the words of our Lord and of St. Paul are stubborn and will not dissolve. The Christian must seek a third solution. Let us first throw a glance at the two wrongheaded attempts to solve the paradox.

It is well to be in the fashion, but, for those who are not, it is a comfort to remember that not every fashion is new. Long skirts and beards return to take their revenge and the fun out of the old family-album. It is much the same in the world of ideas—though ideas do not die even for a time, they live and lurk. Until recently it was the fashion to let the Old Testament die, either under the knife or under gas. This fashion is not new. It is as old as the Seven Hills where Marcion walked and was condemned. And this was (almost to the year) eighteen hundred years ago. "Now then, Marcion", cried Tertullian on the Church's behalf, "you and your axe—get out of my plantation!" (Though here I should mention, to defend the dignity of this great lawyer, that his own words were more formal—not less strenuous however: "Quo denique, Marcion, iure sylvam meam caedis?" *De Praescrip.*, 37.) Marcion's axe had, it is true, cut down the towering difficulties of the Old Testament but it was by dint of felling the whole forest as the planting of Satan. For Marcion the Old Testament was a powerful thing but an evil thing. The books themselves and the state of things they describe were alike the work of an evil deity, of the god of Wrath. Now the popular answer to-day is the same as Marcion's but surely less striking. Why? Because the modern world is, to its peril, shy of seeing personality in the principle of Evil. It agrees with Marcion because it refuses to believe that it is the same God who speaks "in times past by the prophets, in these days by his Son" (Heb. i. 1). Observe now the consequences of the policy. Marcion very soon found that his axe brought down most of the New Testament also. It left standing only ten of the Epistles of Paul together with a mutilated trunk of St. Luke's Gospel. Marcion's logic (a rare bird to-day) was faultless and ruthless. Let him stand for a warning: it may well prove that the Old Testament and the New are set too close for separate slaughter.

It takes two to make a quarrel. Marcion had stopped the fight by pitching the Old Testament out of the ring. The alternative was to eject the New. This the Jew has done. Marcion was wrong but not as wrong as this. We must at least give him the credit for seeing that the Old Testament could not possibly be God's last word to man. The Israelite on the other hand is well satisfied with this record of God's favours to his race because when religion and patriotism kiss they make a strong alliance. The exclusive, national character of the Mosaic Law is for him no scandal. He holds that the world is not even yet ripe for religious internationalism. When that time comes it is Judaism that will be found to have leavened the world. For him the new testament is still being written—in the blood of his persecuted tribe. Israel is the Suffering Servant of God (cf. Isa. lii–liii) and through its endurance the world will attain to salvation. What does the Jew mean by "salvation"? It would be unjust to generalize but certain Jewish thinkers of the day identify it with "social justice". Shylock is, doubtless, a vicious caricature but Jewry has always leaned more to justice than to charity. "Then must the Jew be merciful," says Portia. What says Shylock? "On what compulsion must I? Tell me that . . . I crave the law, The penalty and forfeit of my bond." Nothing but the mighty power of grace will bend this spirit. Meanwhile the gentle message of the New Testament goes unregarded. Yet this mysterious Race remains—a marvel to the world, a witness to the power of Yahweh, a proof that the promises of the Old Testament were not vain. Israel waits. Four thousand years have not drained the patience of the children of Abraham.

Next door to the synagogue stands the Christian church where the sacred Book of the synagogue has its place. The same Book? Yes, but not the same mind that reads and receives. The difference is not slight. Ideas, like water, take the shape of their receptacle. For example, the line: "And no birds sing" is a bald statement of fact for the child but, for the poet, it has the beauty of a dying cadence. When the Christian and the Jew bend over the same Book they read through different eyes. The Christian is the Israelite

B

divinely grown. The Christian mind, matured and enriched by the Sermon on the Mount, reads the unchanging Decalogue itself with a new intelligence. For him the Old Testament has been touched to a new life by the hand of Christist. Like a risen body it is dead and yet it lives, and lives more gloriously; the corruptible has "put on incorruption". The miracle is in the order of mind and spirit but it is not less than the raising of the son of the widow.

This statement of the Christian case is not new. Less than thirty years after our Lord's death St. Paul saw the situation thus:

To this day, I say, when the Law of Moses is read out, a veil hangs over their [the Jews'] *hearts. There must be a turning to the Lord first, and then the veil will be taken away. . . . It is given to us* [Christians] . . . *to catch the glory of the Lord as in a mirror, with faces unveiled.* (2 Cor. iii. 14–18. Knox Version.)

From a slightly different standpoint the epistle to the Hebrews speaks of:

A new and living way which he [our Lord] *has dedicated for us through the veil.* (Heb. x. 20.)

The Temple-veil was rent when our Lord died. It was not without significance: he has penetrated the veil of old Sanctuary and old Scripture at once.

The Christian should not, through laziness, selfishness or contempt, watch the Jewish and the pagan worlds roll by unconcerned. He must make it his business to explain, before Jew and Gentile, how the Old Testament is neither the treasure-chest of all wisdom nor, on the other hand, a box of toys. To the Jew he must try to show that its divine promises have not been delayed, that "the kingdom of God is amongst us", that the fulfilment is no less a fulfilment because it exceeds the wildest words of the promise. To the Gentile he must prove that, if God's Spirit has spoken through his Son, the same Spirit spoke—more faintly but as truly—through the inspired Scribes of Israel. He must show, to both Jew and Gentile, that there is not true discord between the Old and New but a harmony which is resolved in Christ.

II

INSPIRATION AND THE OLD TESTAMENT

OUR PENNY Catechism, excellent in so many other respects, does not deal with the doctrine of Inspiration. It is therefore something of a mystery where many of us Catholics get our notion from. No doubt "the word of God" is a phrase common enough in England; it is on the lips of Catholics and non-Catholics alike. But we have to be careful. Like tobacco or tea, phrases readily take the flavour of their surroundings. It may be that with the phrase "Word of God" we have inhaled something of the rather stale taste of the Reformation—something of the meaning attached to it outside the Church in the sixteenth century, a meaning long since abandoned even by the most stubborn. Few nowadays would subscribe to the old Calvinistic belief that the very consonants and vowel-signs of our present Hebrew text were revealed by God. It would be a tragic irony indeed if the Catholic were to cling to a position never held by the Church and long since deserted even by those outside her fold! Now the matter is so important that we dare take no risks. Let us, then, go forward slowly and carefully together.

Our knowledge of the mysterious actions of God is like the ascending corner-lines of a pyramid whose head is hidden in the clouds. Geometrical calculation will establish the meeting-point which, however, remains invisible. Similarly our ideas of God converge upon the one point and are therefore true *as far as they go*. Yet they cannot be perfect until we come to the eternal Vision. Of these imperfect ideas Inspiration is one. We say that the Bible is "inspired" or "breathed into" by God. Now God is a Spirit. He does not "breathe" as we do. It follows that we are merely using a convenient word for a mysterious divine action of which we can know something but not everything. We can know the effects of it but we cannot completely grasp its inner nature. We are forced back to comparisons, as we shall see in a moment.

Inspiration is *a positive, divine influence upon the intellect and will of the human writers of the sacred books*. But this influence, though it completely pervades those faculties and wields them in their action, does not rob the human writer's intellect of activity nor his will of freedom. May I ask you here to shed your imagination? It will not help but hinder. No human motion is comparable to this. You have been warned that the head of the pyramid is in the clouds. Now this divine influence makes God the principal author of the books while the human writer becomes his instrument. Unlike any other book, therefore, a sacred book has two authors—one "principal", the other "instrumental"; one divine, the other human. There is one divine author of the Bible; there are many human authors. There is one divine author for both Old and New Testaments—not the slightest inequality between Old and New *from this point of view*; one equal inspiration common to both.

We have spoken of the author as an "instrument" of God. Remember that this is a comparison, only a comparison. It was made by the early Fathers and developed by later theologians, particularly by St. Thomas Aquinas in the thirteenth century. (For the sake of the reader anxious for a fuller treatment I must mention that the best little book, to my knowledge, is the commentary on St. Thomas's tract on Prophecy by Fathers Synave and Benoit, O.P. It was published by Desclée in 1947.) Of all comparisons this of the "instrument" is the most useful for understanding our subject. Many theologians of the last century may have allowed it to fall into the background but our present Holy Father has deliberately emphasized the value of this approach in the "liberating Encyclical", the *Divino Afflante* of 1943.

Now the idea of "instrument" cannot mislead if we remember that the human author is not a *dead* instrument. He is not like a piece of dead chalk in the hands of the writer. He is a living thing with its human faculties of intellect and will. He has a memory of his own, a whole series of psychological "associations" of his own, a language and style of his own—and not always a very perfect style at that. Take St. John, for example. I do not imagine that any man of letters would applaud him for the way he joins up his sentences in his gospel. No less than one hundred and ninety-five times (some say two hundred times) he uses "therefore" to do so! One involuntarily thinks of a child telling a story—count the number of times he says "then"! But, to resume: in the hands of God, so powerful and yet so delicate, this "instrument" is moved, probably unconsciously as a rule, as if it were a living and thinking pastel. It follows that what we may call the "colour" of the pastel, and by that I mean the distinctive characteristics of the human author, will be recognizable on the canvas. Isaias the courtier, Amos the shepherd, Mark the diarist, John the contemplative—all speak their own language.

In other words, the inspired writer is not a kind of gramophone upon which God places his ready-made records. The Church has never thought so. So then, without regret, let us carry to the grave the "verbal dictation" theory of the early Reformers with every single one of its tattered trappings.

There can be no formal error in the inspired books. By

formal error, it should be remarked *en passant*, we mean error which the author makes his own; he may, for instance, quote an erroneous statement ("There is no God") while disclaiming responsibility for it ("The fool hath said in his heart: There is no God"). This quality of "inerrancy", as it is called, necessarily follows from "Inspiration" as we have defined and described it. Why? Because God remains ultimately responsible despite his use of an "instrument". What would you think if your little pupil blamed his grammar mistakes on his naughty pen? His bad writing, yes; his mistakes, no. But we shall not speak of "mistakes" yet—we shall do our best to vindicate the Bible from these later on. We must first give some indication of the importance and wide application of this "defective instrument" principle.

Pope Pius XII in the Encyclical we have mentioned is careful to call the inspired book "the fruit of his [the human author's] labour" in which we may recognize his "distinctive genius and individual characteristics". Now remember: these "individual characteristics" could not possibly include a habit of making mistakes or of telling lies. This is already cut out by what we have said in the preceding paragraph. Very well, then, we can go safely on to illustrate this principle with practical examples.

Did our Lord teach his disciples the "Our Father" right at the beginning of his public life or towards the end? St. Matthew puts it at the beginning—in the inaugural discourse which we call the Sermon on the Mount (cf. Matt. v. 3–13). St. Luke on the other hand places it at the time of our Lord's journey to Jerusalem and to his Passion (Luke xi. 2–4). Each evangelist is following his particular bent. Luke is the historian who, when he is certain of the order of events in *time*, prefers that order. Matthew is a historian too, but he prefers a grouping of *ideas*; consequently, when our Lord speaks of prayer in the Sermon

Matthew deems it a suitable place for the ideal prayer. Some modern history-books adopt a somewhat similar procedure. In this case, therefore, we make allowance for the cast of mind of the human authors. Matthew and Luke do not contradict one another but, if we seek the chronological order, we give the preference to Luke. With this order Matthew was simply not concerned. But as to the wording of the prayer itself we prefer and use Matthew's form which is longer than Luke's. Why? Because Luke was an abbreviator by nature.

Or take St. John. Here is a contemplative soul writing in old age. Years of meditation on his Master's words often lead him to present the sense of those words in his own very marked vocabulary and style (e.g. John iii. 16–21). In all such cases the prudent interpreter will have to see to it that he appreciates these "individual characteristics" of the human author. As the Holy Father says, "he will thus be able better to discover who the sacred author was and what he meant by what he wrote". Nor will he be hasty, as many have been hasty, to conclude that a slightly different form given to our Lord's words in the different evangelists justifies our asserting that the words were repeated on different occasions. Perhaps they were, but this will have to be proved on other grounds.

When we pass to the Old Testament the business of ascertaining "individual characteristics" is even more delicate because (again to quote the *Divino Afflante*) "it is absolutely necessary for the interpreter to go back in spirit to those remote centuries of the East". And how remote they are! More remote in literary fashion than in time, though we are coming to learn more every year. To take but one example—the habits of Semitic historians. Over forty years ago a Semitic scholar (Guidi in the *Revue Biblique* for 1906; pp. 509–519) pointed out what is, for us, a most uncomfortable habit of the Semitic historian.

Of course we do not expect, and we do not get, the modern practice of copious reference to sources; but what we are not prepared for is the quoting of those sources without the slightest explicit indication that we are in the presence of a quotation. Now presumably when an author quotes a document he approves of it—at least in its general sense—unless, of course, he gives indications to the contrary. If an inspired author approves then God approves; there can be no formal error and that is the end of it. But suppose an inspired author uses two documents whose presence is betrayed only by a difference of style and approach. Suppose that he incorporates each without change. What, then, of the "individual characteristics" of the inspired author? Surely they are borrowed, in this case, from the original authors. The inspired author makes these characteristics his own; it is therefore these characteristics we shall be forced to examine. One of the original authors may have been a historian, for instance, of Luke's disposition, another of Matthew's. This one book with two voices will have to receive the benefit we have allowed to the two separate books of Matthew and Luke. Shall we have an example for clarity's sake?

It is, to say the least, highly probable that the inspired author of Genesis has used one document for the story of Creation (i. 1–ii. 4), another for the story of the Fall (ii. 4–iii. 24) which includes (ii. 4–ii. 24) a second description of Creation. Now the order of Creation differs in the two accounts. In the first account Man appears at the end (like the "Our Father" in Luke); in the second he appears at the beginning (like the "Our Father" in Matthew). Is this contradiction? We might think so if one author with one mentality were responsible for the original accounts but here, it seems, we have two separate mentalities, two different points of view to take into consideration. Neither is concerned with the chronology of

Creation but the first, true to his logical sense, puts the most perfect creature last; the second, eager to show how all other creatures were made for Man, presents him to us at the outset, standing complacently by while God creates his toys for him.

Now perhaps you have been surprised at the very idea of an inspired writer quoting or using at length some uninspired author or document. If so, we must again insist that the inspired author is not a passive puppet.

All such things as have been comprised in five books by Jason of Cyrene we have attempted to abridge in one book . . . in undertaking this work of abridging we have taken in hand no easy task, yea rather a business full of watching and sweat. (2 Mach. ii. 24, 27.)

Does this sound like inactivity? Does it seem that God has poured the ideas into the writer's head? No. Yet the work is inspired? Yes. Well, then, inspiration does not necessarily mean the infusion of new ideas by God. This is only another way of saying that *inspiration is not the same thing as revelation.* It should, however, be noticed that we use the word "revelation" in the modern sense—the divine manifestation of a truth hitherto unknown. To avoid confusion it must be mentioned that the term has a wider sense, frequently used by Aquinas for instance, of "a divinely guaranteed statement". This is the meaning we give to the expression when we say that the whole Bible is "revelation". But we shall use the word in the narrower, modern, sense throughout. Let us repeat, then: when God *inspires* he does not necessarily *reveal*; he simply gives his divine garantee to what has been written or (more accurately) his guarantee is implicit in the whole motion of inspiration which precedes and accompanies the act of writing. The second book of Machabees is an inspired summary of the five uninspired books of Jason. The facts assumed into the summary, in the sense in which they *are* assumed and made his own by the inspired writer, now have a divine guarantee which they did not enjoy before. The distinction we have drawn is important. Let us have a few examples. Here is a sentence *inspired but not revealed*:

From that hour the disciple took her into his own keeping.

St. John (xix. 27) needed no revelation from God to remind him that he had taken care of Mary and God's wisdom is essentially economic; it does not multiply without necessity. We cannot, therefore, assume revelation here. Nevertheless, the sentence is part of the inspired gospel of John. Here now is a sentence with both *inspiration and revelation*:

And when the seventy years shall be expired, I will punish the king of Babylon. (Jer. xxv. 12.)

Jeremias could not have foretold the length of the Babylonian captivity without revelation. This revelation is committed to writing by an inspired writer. The third and last example does not, on this count, concern the Scripture scholar but we add it for completeness' sake. It is a sentence *without inspiration but with revelation*:

We declare, proclaim and define that the doctrine maintaining that the most blessed Virgin Mary was preserved from all stain of original sin is a doctrine revealed by God. (Bull *Ineffabilis*, 1854.)

The most solemn pronouncements of the Holy Father or of the Councils are not inspired. They are infallible. That is to say, they have a negative assistance from God which guards them from error. Inspiration, too, guards a writer from error but this is far from being its only purpose. Moreover, inspiration is a positive influx and not merely a negative assistance. I say that inerrancy is not the only purpose of Inspiration. By this I mean that the inspired is not out to make a continuous series of explicit and naked affirmations. He often seeks to decorate his truth (for nothing but truth can underlie his work) with picturesque phrases or images which are not statements but ornaments. This happens particularly in elevated style—in exhortation, dire threat and the rest. Such phrases are not to be amputated from the body of their context and scrutinized in isolation as if of themselves they were living organisms. They live only with the life of the whole. That is to say, they help to convey the truth of the whole which is implicit in them. But they do not enjoy the status of independent assertions. It follows that the single terms of such phrases are not to be weighed beyond the measure which the author's context confers upon them. Let us take a simple example. When the psalmist laments:

The Lord hath looked down from heaven upon the children of men to see if there be any that understand and seek God . . . there is none that doth good, no not one. (Ps. xiii. 3f.)

he bewails, indeed, a general apostasy. This is the truth implied in the words; were there no such apostasy the inspired author would be in error. It would be foolish, however, to argue from the phrase: "No, not one" that the psalmist's words would be falsified by a single exception. Yet every single word of Scripture is inspired! The solution is that the choice of this rhetorical phrase is governed, to put it technically, rather by the practical judgment than by the speculative. The speculative judgment is concerned with the underlying truth, the practical with its mode of presentation. In our example, if we consider the emphatic, rhetorical phrase as a separate entity, Inspiration guarantees the soundness of the author's choice of this hyperbolical expression to secure his purpose —it operates on his practical judgment. In this case, as in many similar, the purpose of Inspiration is not inerrancy but emphasis which, so long as it is a truth which is thus legitimately emphasized, is all we look for in hyperbolical turns of speech. The underlying truth is, of course, the product of the speculative judgment which alone is capable of truth or error. Inspiration of the speculative judgment ensures truth.

This is all very interesting, the reader may say, but where does all your fine theorizing come from? How do you know what inspiration is? How do you know that this or that book is inspired? It seems fairly clear that the writer himself was not aware of his own "inspiration". As you and I cannot *feel* sanctifying grace neither could the inspired author *feel* that other kind of grace which is called "inspiration". In fact his tone often positively suggests this ignorance. Take this, for example, from one of the inspired books:

Let this be enough by way of preface: for it is a foolish thing to make a long prologue and to be short in the story itself. (2 Mach. ii. 33.)

Why, the tone is almost playful; certainly it has not the solemnity we should expect from a consciously inspired author. But, if the author cannot tell us, perhaps the sublimity of his work speaks for him? Well, in a sense, it does—especially if his book be considered in its whole literary context of the Bible at large. But if we seek assurance of inspiration in the sense in which we have described it and if we wish to establish the quality of inspiration for every part of the sacred books we shall find this

criterion inadequate. Try reading the thousand and more
names in the first nine chapters of First Paralipomenon
(First Chronicles)! Or take the wisdom of the book of
Proverbs which is shrewd enough but not above man's
unaided capacity:

> *As the door turneth upon its hinges*
> *So doth the slothful upon his bed.* (Prov. xxvi. 14.)

or:

> *A golden ring in a swine's snout*
> *A woman fair and foolish.* (Prov. xi. 22.)

And, in truth, I think you will have guessed by now that to
seek such a criterion is to make that very mistake we have
called attention to: I mean the confusion of inspiration
with revelation.

Neither the author, then, nor the books provide their
own evidence of the fact of inspiration. This must be
firmly stated as against the position taken up by the early
Reformers. It might not be worth stressing were the
position entirely abandoned to-day; but it is not. It lingers
on in the Report of the 1922 Commission dealing with
"Doctrine in the Church of England", though with
modifications in the right direction. It may be found
underlying an admirable exposition of "The authority of
the Bible" by a distinguished professor of divinity at
Cambridge (C. H. Dodd; 1938). Once given the severance
from ecclesiastical authority which was the pivot of the
Reformation movement, the Bible was inevitably isolated.
It was forced to stand on its own legs and to speak for
itself. It had no external support. Since then the peril has
been sensed. Zahn, the great Protestant theologian of the
last century, appealed to early tradition to support the
authority of the Bible. His brilliant young contemporary,

the liberal Protestant Adolf Harnack, saw very clearly what this meant. He exclaimed: "Such an approach would force us to become Catholics!" (cf. Lagrange, *Histoire Ancienne du Canon du Nouveau Testament*, 1933, p. 3).

And it is true that if the author and the books themselves fail us in this matter, as they do, there remains only the explicit revelation of God. Now you and I know that he has not whispered this secret directly to our souls. If therefore he has revealed it at all, the fact of inspiration must have been revealed to God's society which we call the "Church". This appears to be the only logical position. It is difficult indeed to understand the mind of those who accept the Church's books while rejecting the Church's authority.

III

THE DIFFICULTIES OF OLD TESTAMENT INTERPRETATION

WILLIAM TYNDALE wrote to a contemporary theologian in 1520:

> If God spare my life, ere many years I will cause a boy that driveth the plough shall know more of the Scripture than thou dost.

But St. Jerome had written to Paulinus in 394:

> Everyone knows that trades like farming, building, engineering, carpentry, all need apprenticeship. But when it comes to the trade of interpreting the Word of God—well, any talkative old grannie, any old fellow in his dotage, any frothy intellectual will blithely dissect and expound it without bothering to take any lessons in it. . . . This is a childish way of going on, this is circus stuff, to set up as master in your own ignorance. Aye, to let my spleen speak ("ut cum stomacho loquar "!), it means that you don't even know what you don't know.

Our heart may leap out to the ambition of Tyndale but the commonsense and forthright Jerome must have our head. It is the devil who dresses Prudence as the Cinderella of the virtues but Jerome knew the size of her slipper. Time, surely, has vindicated his caution. After centuries of biblical discussion no honest man can fail to feel that something has gone wrong. We are for Tyndale if the ploughboy can take a few years off to pick up Hebrew, Greek, archaeology and the rest. But meanwhile who is to do the ploughing? And so our ploughboy must be provided with Tyndale's own translation—and with Tyndale's notes as well. He will then be able to read the words of Balaam (Num. xxiii. 8): "How shall I curse whom God curseth not?" together with the marginal note: *The Pope can tell how.* Or he can study the phrase of Genesis (xxiv. 60): "They blessed Rebekah", with the marginal note: *To bless a man's neighbour is to pray for him and to wish him good, and not to wag two fingers over him.*

Had Mother Church given up the problem of teaching Piers the Plowman his Bible? No, she had done her best; and certainly she gave him all he needed. He saw it painted on the walls of his church and glowing through its windows—a "Rainbow Bible" of a sort. He was familiar enough with the great facts and figures of the sacred history. He heard of them in ballad, he met them on the stage of the miracle-play. Had there been a cinema he would have seen them there.

But, for better or for worse, things have changed since then. All can read the cheaply-printed Bible. Here indeed in England the love of the Bible is traditional; a virtue which, please God, will be rewarded in the end. As lately as 1881, when the Revised New Testament issued from the presses of Oxford and Cambridge, the public interest was intense and one million copies were sold from the Oxford press on the first day. Nor was America backward. Five days after the English publication two Chicago newspapers printed the entire book as a supplement to their ordinary issue; one half of the text had been received by telegraph before actual copies were available. (The tale is told by Kenyon, *Story of the Bible*, p. 87.)

And yet all is not gain. Perhaps the Bible has as much to fear from the arms of its lovers as from the armament of its enemies. Gilbert Chesterton remarks somewhere that the Mormon reads his Bible and finds polygamy, while the Christian Scientist reads his and finds we have no arms or legs. Sincerity, it would seem, is not enough because sincerity has yielded a thousand contradictory systems. It is evident that we need a guide in these matters. For the moment I do not refer to the authority of the Church but rather to the guidance afforded us by reasoned principles of interpretation, the result of centuries of devoted scholarship and, in more than one case, the happy issue of bitter controversy. The Galileo business, for example, served to bring out the importance of the rule formulated by St. Thomas four hundred years earlier, namely, that in the Scriptures God speaks to men in human fashion. But before we go further it might be as well to state, very briefly, the Catholic's position *vis-à-vis* the Church and the Bible.

For the Catholic the Church's authority is final in the interpretation of the Word of God. This is not to say that the Church's interpretation meets the scholar at every turn. Far from it. Our present Holy Father writes in the *Divino Afflante*:

The rules and laws laid down by the Church (i.e. rules and laws connected with the science of interpretation) are concerned with the doctrine of faith and morals; and amongst the many matters set forth in the legal, historical, sapiential and prophetical books of the Bible *there are only a few* whose sense has been declared by the authority of the Church, and there are equally few concerning which the opinion of the holy Fathers is unanimous (and therefore binding). (CTS. trans. The two parentheses and the italics are ours.)

The number of texts which have been solemnly interpreted by the Church is little more than one dozen though, of course, one must not forget the implicit interpretations which are latent in her practice. When Scripture texts contain matters of faith or morals the Church's power to interpret them is known as "direct and positive". This means that she is immediately and legitimately concerned with their content for its own sake and is competent not merely to exclude false interpretations but to propose and impose the right one. Over other texts (containing history, science, etc.), it is clear from the discussions at the Vatican Council that here, too, she claims authority. This power, however, is called "indirect and negative". It is indirect because it is not concerned with the content of the text for its own sake (the content is not in itself religious) but with safeguarding the dogma of inspiration and of inerrancy, its consequence. It is negative because it does not propose one interpretation but merely excludes those which she sees to be incompatible with the dogma of inspiration or inerrancy. Perhaps when our non-Catholic neighbours come to understand the economy of this second claim they will come also to realize that the Catholic Scripture scholar is not bound hand and foot. "There remain many matters, *and important matters*", the Pope goes on, "in the exposition and explanation of which the sagacity and ingenuity of Catholic interpreters can and ought to be freely exercised, so that each in the measure of his powers may contribute to the utility of all, to the constant advancement of sacred learning, and to the defence and honour of the Church."

Well, then, let us not be shy of applying reasoned principles to the Word of God. Why should we? The Saviour of East and West chose to dwell midway between New York and Tokyo. He addressed Pilate, no doubt, in Greek which was familiar to many in Palestine and heard especially in Galilee, but for the most part he accepted the limitations of Palestinian Aramaic. God's written Word, like God's incarnate Word, accepts its limitations. It is written in the tongues of men and, in its defence, man must take up the weapons of reason. The least we claim for the Bible is the justice that would be conceded to any book.

Shall we have this in italics? It is a principle at once obvious, important and forgotten. *The goal of all interpretation is to discover the meaning the author truly intends to convey and truly conveys*. We are not interested, therefore, in what we should *like* the author to say or in what translators or commentators or hecklers try to *make* him say. Good; now we can go on.

Words are dangerous customers. Take the phrase "Beat it!" (if you will excuse me). I shall refuse to tell you what it means until you first let me know whether you met it in rough conversation or in a cookery-book. Again: I suppose "deep" is the opposite of "shallow". I wonder? When the Samaritan woman called Jacob's well "deep" she meant that the water was a long way down ("and you have nothing to draw with"). If, as is very likely, the incident took place in June there was probably very little water in the well. It was, in effect, "shallow". Or again: a few minutes ago I was reading the following sentence: "Herod died in 4 B.C."; only a few pages later I read: "It is quite certain that Herod died in 44 A.D.". Misprint? Mistake? Not a bit of it. Just two different Herods ("the Great" and Agrippa I). Now if this sort of thing can happen in English, what are we to say about a language like Hebrew, still imperfectly known? Take the syntax of the verb; take a rather random and flimsy instance. In our older Breviary we used to recite: "Let God arise . . .". The new Psalter of 1945 has: "God doth arise . . .". The difference of meaning turns upon the position of one small dot and this position was evidently different in the different manuscripts. How are we to decide? By a more profound study of Hebrew syntax which in this case, though it may be rash to say so, appears to favour the older translation. Perhaps we should go back on our tracks. This at least is the opinion of E. Podechard judging on the evidence of versions, syntax and context (Ps. lxvii. 1; cf. *Revue Biblique*, 1947, p. 504).

Or consider the imperfect word-division of the Hebrew manuscripts which can turn: "How kind is God to the just man!" (. . . *lysr 'l*) into: "How kind is God to Israel!" (. . . *lysr'l*). Or the original absence of vowel-points: the term *dabar*, for example, was written *dbr* and in this state besides being capable of representing many parts of the verb "to say" it may mean "word", "pestilence", "pasture". Even if written *dabar* confusion is still possible between the meaning "word" and "thing" and this confusion has seeped into the New Testament in the well-known sentence: "Let us go over to Bethlehem and see this word (i.e. thing) that has come to pass."

Many, many instances might be given; these are examples taken at random. They are meant to induce not despair but caution. They are meant for the bluff-and-blunt method of interpretation which insists on calling a spade a spade only to discover, in five cases out of ten, that it is a shovel after all.

A well-thumbed passage must serve for an example of what we have said regarding the meaning that the author truly intends to convey. But before we come to it, it would be well to make two remarks. First: in the epoch-making Encyclical we have quoted so often and which we shall quote many times again our Holy Father praises the progress made in Catholic circles by the prudent use of modern weapons of learning. Among these he numbers the more profound understanding of the doctrine of inspiration, the new information provided by archaeology, ancient history, the study of ancient literature with its literary methods, forms and devices. He then sets his sure shield

around those Catholic scholars who fight at the forefront
of the battle with courage and skill and the risk of wounds:

Let all other children of the Church . . . avoid that somewhat indiscreet zeal which considers everything new to be
for that very reason a fit object for attack or suspicion.

The second remark is this: the Catholic interpreter is not
out to obliterate certain of the bright pictures of our
younger days; nor does he assume that everything new is
true or that everything ingenious is, by that very quality,
proved; nor is he bent on "making things easier"; nor
does he intend to impose his interpretation but rather to
suggest it. His absorbing purpose is *to discover what the
inspired author means to say.*

With these considerations well in mind we are free to
address ourselves to the crossing of the Red Sea:

The water was as a wall on their right hand and on their left.
(Exod. xiv. 22, 29.)[1]

Two high crystalline walls? Possibly. But does the inspired author mean this? It is very doubtful. True, our
sentence is taken from the prose account and we do not
intend to claim for it the privileges of the poetic form with
which it is clothed in the Canticle of Moses (Exod. xv. 5)
and in the Psalms (Ps. cxxxv. 15). But it is precisely the
prose account that goes out of its way to tell us that the
miracle was worked by means of a "strong east [not
'burning'] wind blowing all the night". This suggests
no sudden arrest of water but rather a gradual, if rapid,
process which does not hint at vertical walls of water. I
doubt if the text as it stands gives us the right to deduce
more than the recession and return of a tidal wave of some

[1] The Hebrew text omits the word " as ".

sort, not uncommon in sandy places. I have stood on the railway platform at Grange-over-Sands and watched such a wave advancing with the speed and depth sufficient to overwhelm an armed host.

But the text says "Wall". Am I sure? The Hebrew word used is *Chomah*, from the verb *chamah* meaning "to protect". It is often used to mean "wall", that is true, but sometimes it means no more than "protection". Thus on one occasion (1 Kings xxv. 16) Abigail's servant told her how David's men had been a "wall" (*chomah*) to their flock—a "protection", of course. The meaning of the inspired author, therefore, may well be this: the water prevented any outflanking movement by the Egyptian squadron and the speed, violence, depth of its return was enough to overtake, overpower, overwhelm it. In any case, the doubt is sufficient to prevent our identifying the pictures in our "Bible Histories" of long ago with the definitions of the Church.

While we are on the subject of walls we may recall another famous wall you remember very well:

The walls [of Jericho] *forthwith fell down.* (Josue vi. 20.)

A few years ago Canon van Hoonacker, a distinguished Catholic exegete (cf. *Vivre et Penser*, 1943–44, p. 305) proposed the following translation:

The garrison collapsed on the spot.

Taking advantage of the wide meaning of *chomah*, as we have done for the Exodus passage, he suggests that the monotony of the sustained perambulation round the town with all the apparatus of Ark, trumpets and war-cry, wore down the nerves of the superstitious inhabitants of Jericho. Hmmmm! Yet if we take the trouble to analyse our spontaneous objection we shall probably find that it

springs from the translation we have been used to—
whereas it is precisely this translation which is under
discussion. Let us notice once more that we are dealing
only with a *suggestion*, but before we reject it altogether we
shall have to offer an alternative solution to the following
difficulties: Rahab's house, *built upon the walls* (thus the
Hebrew text of Josue ii. 15) of the town, was still standing
after the capture of the town (Josue vi. 22ff.); moreover,
the town of Hai fell by stratagem rather than by storm
and yet its fate is compared with that of Jericho (Josue
viii. 2)—and so on.

But it all shows, doesn't it, the delicacy and danger of
translation? Some have rushed to conclusions, for instance, about the phrase: "the brothers of the Lord"
without stopping to ask whether the original Aramaic
term (or the Greek, for that matter) cannot include more
distant relations like cousins. You see, words catch
diseases so easily—I mean that we so often contaminate
them with our own pet ideas. Since our childhood days
the word "angel" has been accumulating fluff and
feathers. This is just our way of picturing beauty and
speed and, no doubt, is all to the good so long as we
remember that we are dealing in symbols. For more
sophisticated minds it might be better to re-translate the
word as "messenger", though even this suggests a bicycle
and basket. At the expense of our intellect the imagination clamours for satisfaction where satisfaction is impossible. We are not content to know that an angel is a
real but entirely spiritual, and therefore unimaginable,
being. We are more interested in the form which he may
temporarily have assumed. More often in the Bible angels
take human form but not always. When the Lord sends
an "angel" to destroy Sennacherib's force (4 Kings xix.
35), are we sure what shape this "messenger" takes?
Probably that of a providential plague.

IV

LITERARY FORMS AND TRUTH

We go upon the practical mode of teaching, Nickleby; the regular education system. C-l-e-a-n, clean, verb active, to make bright, to scour. W-i-n, win; d-e-r, der; winder, a casement. When the boy knows this out of a book, he goes and does it. (NICHOLAS NICKLEBY.)

TO BE SURE education takes many shapes and, as poor Nicholas found, at Dotheboys Hall it took a very practical shape indeed. This is not to say that it was altogether a bad shape. The boys would learn more, at any rate, from the cleaning than from Dr. Squeers' spelling.

In this gentler age the town-child learns much about a cow, for example, from a bright picture and a glass of cream. He is closer to the truth than the adult who knows, alas! that a cow is a horned and domesticated quadruped in some way responsible for his tin of dried milk. The shortest cut to the child-mind is through the eyes and stomach. We were not created as disembodied intelligences; our minds must be coaxed. Truth must go in beauty or she will go unregarded. I do not say that the beauty must be absolute (if there is such a thing on earth). The child's picture-cow may be a gaudy and unlovely cow, yet if it teaches the infant to know a real cow when he sees one his picture is, to this extent, as good as an Old Master.

And before we pass from this point it might be as well to note that even the smallest child is quick to recognize

what is essential in his picture and what is merely orna-
mental. He will not howl with dismay when the cow in
the field does not turn out to be red, white and blue. Nor
will he indignantly cry that his rag-book artist was either
knave or fool. As for the artist himself, whether pictorial
or literary, he is allowed his conventional tricks and enjoys
the right to expect that the convention be recognized as
such and due account taken of it. An artist, of course, may
choose to work outside a convention; I am told that when
Picasso was asked for the names of modern painters he
answered "Moi". In such a case the artist must be prepared to have his work taken at its face-value. Let us also
remember, since we are to deal with a literature that
covers a thousand years at least, that just as ideas of
beauty develop in the human individual so do they in
the human race. Literary conventions change, too: not a
little of Shakespeare is offensive on the modern stage.

We are speaking of a matter of Form. Truth is clothed
in all the motley of the jester's coat: patches of prose and
poetry, fragments of fable, strips of allegory, parable,
historical fiction and the rest. The important thing to
remember is that *each literary form has its own type of truth.*
Not, notice, truth more or less diluted with falsehood but
truth presented more or less directly, more or less baldly.
As for the form itself, this cannot be said to be either true
or false, because it is not a judgment. The form may be
beautiful or ugly, no more. But underlying the form there
is, unless we are in the Jabberwocky-Nonsense-World, an
intention to convey a message. How deep this message
lies will depend upon the nature of the literary form
chosen. We shall have to strike lightly with the spade; its
extraction may prove difficult and its appearance surprising. Consider this line:

Hail to thee, blithe spirit; bird thou never wert!

You know, I have an uneasy feeling that, in the year five thousand and thirteen, some neo-German school of thought will deduce from this line the ornithological ignorance of the second millennium English. But, cheer up, no doubt some rival Academy (more prudent but just as wrong) will hasten to explain that the term "wert", unlike the word "wast", holds a *nuance* of "appearance" as opposed to actual identity. By both schools poor Shelley would be struck dumb; we must speak for him. His lovely, living line has not been even vivisected by our hypothetical critics; it has been murdered and subjected to autopsy; it lies on the marble of the morgue. Oh, surely poetry has its freedoms! It is to be regretted, perhaps, that the poet did not address his skylark by its proper name; that he did not open his ode with the fine, if brief, line: "Alauda Arvensis!" Instead he opened it with a flat lie—and so got nearer the truth.

Because, we must observe, there *is* a truth that the poet wishes to convey. Metaphor and the rest absolves no one from this, though Mr. Hopkinson M.P. once chose to think so at Lord Beaverbrook's expense:

Mr. H: Mr. Churchill has appointed a public man whose slimy trail has crossed the public life of our country for the last thirty years.
The Speaker: I must ask Mr. Hopkinson to moderate his language.
Mr. H: I think I am entitled to use metaphor, and I am speaking purely metaphorically.

Of course he was. He did not mean that Lord B. had horns and a shell. But he did mean something, didn't he?

A dead horse soundly flogged? Perhaps. But the principle we are urging is of great moment for Old Testament interpretation in particular and the Holy Father has recently thought it opportune for emphasis:

A knowledge and careful appreciation of ancient modes of expression and literary forms and styles will provide a solution to many of the objections made against the truth and historical accuracy of Holy Writ.

This on the negative side. On the positive:

[This knowledge] will contribute with equal profit to a fuller and clearer perception of the mind of the sacred author. (*Divino Afflante*, CTS. trans. par. 42.)

Let us begin with a very familiar literary form, poetry. You and I are used to it and have learned to make the necessary allowances for the form chosen. But perhaps we have not realized that we must make the same allowances when we come to interpret the poems of the Bible—and there are so many!

When Israel left Egypt . . . the hills jumped like rams. (Ps. cxiii. 1, 4.)

Did they? Or is it not rather the poet's way of saying: "Israel's joy spread itself, as it were, to the whole of creation" (and what a beautiful line of poetry *that* would make!)? Let us be reasonable! Or again, and this time from a prose book:

When the sun shone upon the shields . . . the mountains glittered therewith and they shone like lamps of fire. (1 Mach. vi. 39.)

The writer certainly would not have us imagine the glass mountains of the fairy-tales.

All this, being obvious, may be deemed useless but that it prepares us to make the necessary allowances where perhaps they have not been made before:

He shook off Pharaoh and his host into the Red Sea. (Ps. cxxxv. 15.)

Or, still more graphically:

They [Pharaoh's host] *are sunk to the bottom like a stone.*
Exod. xv. 5.)

But according to the inspired *prose* account (Exod. xiv. 22–8) the host did not "sink to the bottom" at all. It stayed on the bottom and the returning sea did the rest. You see, the poet has a right to take liberties and a right to expect sympathetic understanding. Hymns like the Psalm and like the Canticle of Moses (Exod. xv. 1–19) have no pretence to historical detail—it is *not the author's intention.* Why, our own Catholic hymns would not be free of grave difficulty were we to refuse this elementary right to the poet:

For the heaven he left he found heaven in thee.

Even as we sing it our Catholic minds, like Fr. Faber's own mind when he composed it, make all the necessary allowances. We know very well that the divine Son could not strictly be said to "leave" heaven. Had Fr. Faber been writing a text-book of theology he would never have used the expression. Now I do not mean to say that we can find such alarming examples in the inspired books but *if* we were to find them, what bottles of Catholic ink would have to be spilt! And all because someone will have forgotten a primary rule of reasoned interpretation.

A little by the way, may I call your attention to a trick of language connected with the text we have just quoted from Psalm cxxxv? Was the pharaoh really drowned? The prose account does not say so, nor does the Canticle of Moses. In this latter case the Douay version reads wrongly: "Pharaoh went in on horseback . . . into the sea". The text should read: "The cavalry of Pharaoh went in ... into the sea". Yet the psalm, at first sight, gives that impression. But probably you remember a thick, black, albeit cheerful, newspaper headline: Rommel On The Run. Only the children saw him with jacket-tails flying. For all we grown-ups knew, Rommel was in a bathchair or in his grave and the statement still remained true. The general and his army, like the king and his kingdom, make a moral unit. In civilizations where the king assumes into his person all the powers of the State such an identification is inevitable. Thus in Daniel vii. 6 and vii. 17 Alexander's *kingdom* is compared to a leopard though it is Alexander himself who, for the swiftness of his march, was the leopard. If the king's army is defeated, it is therefore the "king" who is defeated though he remain at home safe and sound. This figure of speech is common enough even in prose; it is particularly welcome to the rough-cut epic poetry of the Semite. What then if we possess the mummy of the pharaoh Merneptah without a trace of sea-water, say the experts, in its composition? Does this mean that Merneptah could not have been the pursuing pharaoh of the Exodus? It does not. The expression used by the psalmist does not justify this conclusion. It is on quite other grounds that many hold the pharaoh of the Exodus to have been not Merneptah but Amenhotep II who lived two hundred years earlier (1448–1420 B.C.).

But we were observing that allowance must be made for poetic form. Now, though it is not usual to mention it in this connection, this principle plays some part at least in understanding certain rather shocking "imprecations" on the part of the inspired Old Testament authors:

O daughter of Babylon . . . blessed be he that shall take and dash thy little ones against the rock! (Ps. cxxxvi. 8, 9.)

The mind of the man is set upon the defeat of the oppressor Power; the mind of the *poet* paints that defeat. In the practice of the period it meant infant-murder (4 Kings viii. 12). The poet uses the grim image as a synonym for defeat. We too have prayed for the discomfiture of our enemies but, unlike the graphic poet, we do not make explicit to ourselves either in word or even in thought how much that defeat implies: rocks yesterday, H-bombs to-day. The difference between the forthright poet and ourselves is largely one of expression. "Frustrate their knavish tricks!", by all means, but we should be honest enough to remember that this frustration is bound to mean trouble and sorrow for someone however delicately phrased our prayer be. Moreover, we must leave room for poetic hyperbole. The example limps, of course, but I for one refuse to take Mr. Belloc too literally when he sings with savage gusto:

> May all my enemies go to hell; Noel, Noel.

Notice that we do not necessarily commend the *good taste* of the author, even of the inspired author. In this regard Inspiration guarantees not beauty of form but truth of substance. So, for instance, a Father Martindale (who likes not fat, he tells us) is instinctively revolted when he reads:

Let my soul be filled as with marrow and with fat! (Ps. lxii. 6.)

Yet I know he appreciates the spiritual substance which these things represent.

While on this point we may risk being a little technical. In our second essay (page 14) we distinguished Inspiration from Revelation and now we have just contrasted "beauty of form" and "truth of substance". It is time we made ourselves clearer even if the process involves, as it does, a few dry definitions. A useful terminology has been recently proposed in the little book of Frs. Synave and Benoit to which we have referred and which cannot be sufficiently recommended. We shall use it here.

The divine influx which we call "Inspiration" moves, without wrenching, the faculties exercised in writing a book. It moves the will of the author, his intellect and his executive faculties. This singular operation leaves the will free and the "intellectual personality" intact. We do not pretend to understand how. Now as activities of the intellect we may distinguish *speculative* judgment from *practical* judgment. The former assesses the truth of a proposition, the second assesses the means best adapted to its proposal to the public. The former may be engaged without any thought of presenting our conclusions to other people but whenever the latter is exercised it is precisely with a view to addressing others. Now this is most important: there are occasions on which a writer or a speaker is not out to teach but, for instance, to exhort or threaten. His audience is already in possession of the facts, it is his business to make them living and vivid. This was often the case with the Prophets. In such a situation it is the practical judgment which is engaged—how best to exhort, threaten etc.; what form to adopt for the book or the speech. The speculative judgment takes a holiday. Since this takes place in the inspired books (and in many parts of them) our definition of Inspiration must take account of it. With this in mind we may make the following distinctions.

1. *Scriptural Inspiration* is God's movement of the human author's will and practical judgment; this movement is directed to the production of a written work. Thus, for instance, when Isaias uses the terms of Phoenician myth (cf. page 101) he pronounces no judgment on their truth or falsity. His speculative judgment is not involved. It is his

practical judgment that has been at work in choosing this form for his message; it is the practical judgment, therefore, which receives the influx of Inspiration. The effect of Inspiration in this case is not to produce a true speculative judgment but to ensure a sound practical judgment on the means well suited to secure his end.

2. *Prophetic Inspiration* is God's illumination of the speculative judgment of a writer or of a speaker. The raw material for the judgment has been gathered, perhaps, by unaided human effort and the judgment itself already made by the unaided human subject but prophetical inspiration confers a new formality upon this judgment. The judgment is, as it were, born again in the human mind by the power of the Spirit. Being God's judgment now, as well as man's, it is not only true but inevitably true. Luke's "fifteenth year of Tiberius Caesar", for example, has more backing than that of historical research; it is not only Luke's judgment but God's.

3. *Prophetic Revelation* is God's communication of a new truth. Normally, of course, this is accompanied by a divine illumination of the speculative judgment enabling the recipient to comprehend that truth (i.e. accompanied by "Prophetic Inspiration"). But it need not be. Baltasar received the revelation (Dan. v) but he needed Daniel's "prophetic inspiration" to explain it to him.

Now in the sacred books what we have numbered '1' is always present, usually '2', sometimes '3' also. When all three are present the sacred writer has received a revelation, understood it and committed it to writing in a suitable form.

c

V

MORE ABOUT LITERARY FORMS. THE CANTICLE

THE MODERN woman of Samaria goes to the well, I am told, not with a pitcher but with a petrol-tin. There is a warning for us here. As you and I potter through these pages we are working together to fashion a pitcher for the living water of Sacred Scripture lest it take the wrong shape and be polluted with an alien spirit. To avoid the risk of exegetical lead-poisoning we are trying to put ourselves in the place of the readers of old for whom the Books were originally meant. We men must change our jacket for a burnous; ye women, the half-veil for the yashmak. There is an easier alternative, not entirely useless at times but dangerous always—I mean to translate the ancients into our own fashions. There is a passage of Zacharias, for example:

Thirty pieces of silver! . . . *A fine price to be assessed at!* . . . *Throw it to the potter!* (Zach. xi. 12ff.)

This fierce scorn of a despised God echoes faintly, you remember, as a sad irony in the Gospel of St. Matthew (xxvii. 9). Now if for the "potter", that is to say the cheap-shop, you and I read "the Woolworth store", we score a point in journalese perhaps and possibly taste the truc flavour of the passage. Yet it is a risky business to force live and kicking limbs into splints for the purposes of observation; or, if you wish, to freeze the living water that we may at leisure admire the beauty of its flow.

On the whole, we shall probably be wiser to don the skins of the ancients, if we can. But they cannot be thrown on like an overcoat; they must be eased on like a lady's glove. And, alas, we are not even yet in the middle of this delicate process. We are still speaking of forms of literature familiar to us. We have not reached the point where we can say: "Ah, here is a literary form strange to modern times!" But, I warn you, we are passing from the more to the less familiar. We are being weaned.

God is the "principal" author of Holy Writ; men were his "instruments". Man has his thought-forms; God has his holiness, his truth, his wisdom. In the total result of this unique co-operation which we call the Bible no form of human literature is necessarily excluded provided that form be not opposed to God's sanctity, truth, wisdom. Thus "myth" is excluded if by "myth" we mean a story essentially involving false notions of the Godhead, though the terms of myth may be turned to very good purpose, as we shall see. What about Fables? Are these opposed to God's *truth*? No. How true is a fable? As true, or false, as its moral. Aesop, surely, was not lying when he made his fox talk. But he would have been lying, or mistaken, had the "sour grapes" principle been false. As for the *sanctity* of God, would a mere love-poem be excluded? Not on this count, provided it were not immoral. It remains to be seen whether it would tell against his *wisdom*. This last attribute, we may presume, will not admit of forms of literature useless to his purpose. "God", said Augustine, "was out to make Christians, not mathematicians." Why, then, should we seek anywhere in the Bible for the literary form (if we may use the expression) of a scientific text-book? Goodness me! Suppose God had forced Moses to speak in terms of Einstein physics! And, if it comes to that, is Einstein's the last word? We may thank God that he did not reveal the whole truth in all its gigantic simplicity. Had he done so, it is highly probable that each succeeding generation, including our own, would have smiled with pity for its absurdity. On the pages of the universe, not of the Bible, God has written his text-book and many, I fear, are reading it who have some vague notion that they are writing it.

Among the fancy-dress parade of literary forms the Parable is clamouring for our notice. He is akin to the Fable though, for the sake of appearances and of human interest, he is dressed nearer to the everyday styles of men. But he is not a dryasdust lecturer either. He has his little pedagogic tricks and we must not always take him too seriously. We need not, for example, rake the botanical specimens of the museums in an effort to prove that the mustard-seed is indeed "the least of all seeds". Nor must we search for a soil that will bring forth precisely "an hundredfold". Nor should we be at all put out if there never had been a real inn on the road from Jericho to Jerusalem. Neither is it wise to make an act of faith in the Jerusalem guides who will undertake (in better times, I hope!) to show us the house of Dives—a building of the Middle Ages! Dives lived in no house: Dives lived in a hundred houses; Dives lived in a parable.

Allegory is the rich relation of Parable. He is often a little over-dressed for our taste. He is sophisticated, too, and very, very cunning. Friendly enough, mind you, but you must hang on his every word—he does not suffer fools gladly. (There! I have unwittingly caught his manner myself!) He betrays himself, deliberately, by his very extravagance. Listen:

> *Thy nose is as the Tower of Libanus . . .*
> *Thy head is like* [Mount] *Carmel.* (Cant. vii. 4f.)

And this in a description of the beautiful bride of the Canticle of Canticles! Really it seems just a little too picturesque and enormous even for Oriental imagery. After all, the "Tower of Libanus" is, with much probability, Great Hermon. It is the Djebel *esh-Sheikh* (i.e. the "Old Man"—as we speak of "Coniston Old Man") of Palestine's northern border. His frosty poll lifts to a height of 9,000 feet! Possessed of a feature comparable to that, is the bride a woman at all? A giantess, surely! Yet, again, beware! Who are we to lay down the law and the boundaries for the ancients? Still, it is small wonder if, confronted with phrases like these, many an exegete has fled down the allegorical track. Allegory of what? I for one cannot resist the invitation, the pressing invitation, of the persistent geographical references and think it not unlikely that the "bride" is Israel in her God-prepared bower, the Holy Land. Israel of whom God had said:

She shall call me: Husband. . . . I will espouse thee to me for ever. (Osee ii. 16, 19.)

If this be so, our whole attitude towards the mysterious Canticle suffers a rich change. From a passionate love-poem ("très poussée", as someone has remarked) it rises almost to the height of Christian mysticism. I say "almost" because, in the Old Testament manner, it is content with the mysticism of God's union with his People *as a whole*. The mystery of his espousals with the individual soul is not fully developed in these terms even in the New. Paul himself is thinking of the Church as a whole when he writes:

I have espoused you to one husband that I may present you as a chaste virgin to Christ. (2 Cor. xi. 2; cf. Eph. v. 25.)

The individual mysticism finds its highest and most mature expression in the writings of contemplatives like Teresa of Avila and John of the Cross.

This allegorical interpretation is further recommended by the fact that it solves a problem. The "naturalist", or "romantic", school which assigns the seven songs of the Canticle to the seven-day celebrations of some human wedding, finds it difficult to explain how a passionate nuptial song slipped into the canon of sacred books despite the vigilance of the Rabbis. The pious and learned Rabbi Aqiba, who died nobly for Judaism in the second century of our era, used to call the Canticle a "holy of holies", that is a most sacred thing, because it celebrated the love of Yahweh for Israel. He was fiercely indignant with those who brazenly sang it as a common love-song in the cabarets.

Nevertheless, it would be absurd to pretend that the interpretation which follows is the only probable one. It is defended by Fr. Joüon S.J. (*Le Cantique des Cantiques*, 1909) and will serve to illustrate what we mean by "allegory".

Have you ever misread a key-signature? Of course you have—and with the most disastrous results. Now the literary form of a book or of a passage is its key-signature. In the case we are considering the whole piece is played in "Allegory" key, with a few accidentals, no doubt, and in that key alone is it harmonious. Unfortunately the composer does not write at the head of his script: "To be played in Allegory", but if its traditional manner of performance *plus* its intrinsic musical satisfaction both point to the Allegory key, surely we are justified in our allegorical interpretation?

For "traditional performance" we have quoted Aqiba but as one only of the many early Jewish interpreters whose opinion the writers of the early Church made their own. As for the internal harmony of the allegorical tone, this is a matter for the sensitive and experienced ear. Later, I hope, we shall develop this ear for ourselves. Meanwhile let us make the following brief observation. Among the tests for Allegory literary tradition is of high importance; a prominent place also must be given to picturesque exaggeration of phrase. But our final test for Allegory is the discovery of an historic situation or of some factual background that will satisfy its terms. This implies a familiarity built up of a thousand little bricks of information. Very, very difficult to acquire for a remote time and place though we have it for our own. So, for instance, you and I would not be thwarted by the language of Victorian melodrama: "So ho, pretty bird! You would use your claws then? You vainly beat those lovely pinions against this cage, my dove!". You will have guessed already that Jasper is not addressing his parrot. You are familiar with the literary form, you see. But, were you not so familiar, the dramatic situation as presented on the stage would make all clear. Jasper, true to form, is allegorizing.

Having said this let us now get back to our Canticle. Let us suppose that it is the religious history and the religious hope of Israel set in allegory—the allegory of lover and beloved. A bold hypothesis? Yes indeed, if such an allegory were an isolated case in Hebrew literature. But it is not. We have already heard Osee telling of God pleading with Israel, his faithless spouse, planning to win her back by the hard way of chastisement and exile:

I will lead her into the wilderness and I will speak to her heart.
(Osee ii. 14.)

Osee's language is robust and his rebuke bitter but he is delicacy and mildness itself if we compare him with Ezechiel who, in his longest chapter (xvi), paints and rates the inconstancy of this ungrateful wife:

And thy renown went forth among the nations for thy beauty: for thou wast perfect through my beauty which I had put upon thee, saith the Lord God. But trusting in thy beauty thou playedst the harlot. (Ezech. xvi. 14f.)

We may find this dark side of the picture shocking and distasteful. It was meant to be shocking; it was not meant to be distasteful but conventions change. In any case we cannot fail to see the surpassing beauty of the image of God's love for his people. It is not surprising that it was laid up in the treasury of Hebrew religious thought. Our Lord brought it out again when he called himself the Bridegroom (Mark ii. 19f.) and when he spoke parabolically of his coming to Israel as the wedding-time for the son of the King (Matt. xxii. 1–14). St. Paul, who had fed on the Scriptures from boyhood, could not resist it:

. . . they shall be two in one flesh. A high mystery this—I am thinking of Christ and his Church. (Eph. v. 31f.)

Our hypothesis is not a wild one therefore. It remains now to apply what we have called the final test for allegory, namely the discovery of a key of fact to fit the lock of fancy. The more intricate and elaborate the fancy, the more smooth the fit of the key, so much the more confident shall we be that we have found the key which was made for the lock, or rather that we have found the key for which the lock was made. At the end of it all we should be able to sit back happily on our heels like a burglar at an opened safe. We should be able to say of our theory: "Too good not to be true." *We* should be able to say? No, others should be able to say. For we are human, alas, and our own geese are swans or, as the Arab less delicately but more quaintly says, every man's own fleas are gazelles. Many an exegete has come along with his key and we have heard it grind in the lock but he has not. Yet if he opens the door at all we should clap and if it is the stubborn door of the Canticle we should cheer—grind or no grind. It is in this sympathetic spirit that we approach Joüon's solution.

It is claimed that the Canticle is an allegorized *history* of Israel's relation to her God. The history itself, like a diptych, presents two panels; these are hinged on the Babylonian exile of the sixth century. The prophets paint it after the following fashion.

First Panel: from her idolatrous inconstancy in Egypt, called "harlotry" by Ezechiel (xxiii. 19), God delivers Israel. He makes her his bride in the desert of Sinai and brings her home to Canaan; the alliance is sealed and solemnized by God's dwelling with her in the first Temple, the Temple of Solomon (cf. 3 Kings viii). But, if we may recall the sixteenth chapter of Ezechiel, Israel fell to faithlessness again.

Second panel: the Bride is punished by captivity in another Egypt which is Babylon this time. But there is a second Exodus, as Isaias likes to call it (Isa. xlii. 13–xliv. 23), and God once more leads his spouse through the desert, the eastern desert, now, back home to Palestine.

So much for the key; now for the lock. It is maintained that the Canticle, too, is hinged; the hinge is said to lie between verses one and two of chapter five. On either side, each leaf of the diptych offers us a picture and the two are strangely like. In each the Bride loses the Groom: "I sought him and found him not" (the same phrase in iii. 1 as in v. 6) and, seeking him, encounters the city-guards (identical Hebrew phrase in iii. 3; v. 7). Twice she is seen "rising from the desert" (iii. 6; viii. 5); twice she invites her spouse to the mountain (ii. 7; viii. 14); twice her beauty is glowingly described—the "hair like a flock of goats" and the "teeth like a flock of sheep" in iv. 1–2 find an exact echo in vi. 4–5. In the first picture the Groom invites the Bride to his country: "Arise, make haste my love, my dove, my beautiful one, and come . . . The flowers have appeared in our land" (ii. 10–12). In the second picture the Bride thus invites her Spouse: "Come, my beloved, let us go forth . . . Let us see if the flowers be ready" (vii. 11–12). If this duality is deliberate it needs explanation; Joüon not unreasonably suggests that the explanation lies in the duality of Israel's history. If this suggestion, which is general in character, be supported by detail, then it may be said to grow in probability.

The Canticle is, of course, more ornate than the prose version of Israel's history. It displays a trialogue form, too, which is not the least of the obstacles to its interpretation. Now it is the Groom who speaks, now the Bride, now the Chorus; the author leaves the identity of the speaker to our commonsense. Yet as the light of the historical situation dawns upon the Canticle it does seem to chase many a dark shadow. We see the royal Bridegroom as the God of Israel; his nuptial pavilion is made, as the temple of Solomon was made, of the wood of Libanus (iii. 9; cf. 3 Kings v. 6ff.). The Bride becomes Israel; the "house of her mother" (viii. 2) the second, post-exilic, temple of the new and enduring nuptials. The Choir is the applauding nations and at times, for literary economy, the inhabitants of Jerusalem. Lesser allegorical elements fall into place too. The Vine, for instance, is the Holy Land and the spiritual kingdom which should flourish there; it recalls the vineyard-allegory of Isaias (chapter v) used by our Lord (Matt. xxi. 33ff.). The sleep of the Bride is Israel's calm enjoyment of her God.

There are individual phrases also which though long familiar have remained mysterious. Certain of these now begin to take intelligible shape. Thus the one who is "black but beautiful" (better "swarthy but beautiful"—

Hebrew has no special word for "brown") is Israel, scorched by the suns and labour of Egypt (i. 4). She may be a mere "flower of the field" as she herself admits (ii. 1) but God's reassuring voice declares that she is "a lily among thorns" (ii. 2); Israel is lovelier to him than the thorns which are the nations. Who, then is she that

cometh forth as the morning rising, fair as the moon, bright as the sun, terrible as an army in battle array?

The People of God rising from their captivity in the east, moving like the sun and moon westwards and homewards at the invitation of the Spouse. Meanwhile the Choir of Nations ideally hails the Bride from Sion in the strangely haunting line:

Return, return, O Sulamite; return, return that we may behold thee!

Both quotations come from the second half of the Canticle (vi. 9, 12). In the hypothesis we have adopted for the purpose of illustrating the allegorical method they refer, therefore, to the return not from Egypt but from Babylon in the east, hence the comparison with the sun's progress. Far-fetched? Of course it is. So is all allegory.

Though it is beyond our immediate scope, we should like the opportunity to pass without a mention of the Church's free and lovely use of the Canticle in our Lady's honour. Such liturgical practice is not, nor is intended to be, a declaration of the inspired author's conscious meaning. Yet the words of the Canticle, dear to the Church for two thousand years, praise the beauty of a spouse of God. This high dignity belongs in its highest sense to the Virgin-spouse of the Holy Ghost. Of her the words become truer than ever. Of Israel, perhaps, they were first used but it is the Church who pays Israel the compliment when she uses them of Mary.

VI

THE LITERARY FORM OF THE BOOK OF JONAS

Then ranne the dogge before . . . and . . . with the fawning of his tayle reioyfed. (*It nothing difgraceth the facred hiftorie that a fmal matter being alfo true is recorded with the reft.*)

Tobias xi. 9. (Original Douay with note).

TOBIAS's dog would have blushed to know his fame. You can see that he was distinguished with a note all to himself in the Douay of 1609. He achieved special mention in the last century, too. When some suggested that he might be evicted from the Inspiration in which he was enshrined the Church herself took his part—in very general terms of course, but the issue was far from trivial. It involved the whole question of the extent of Inspiration. To those who would restrict Inspiration to matters of faith and morals the encyclical *Providentissimus Deus* (1893) replied with a firm "no!" (cf. Denzinger-Bannwart, *Enchiridion Symbolorum*, 1950). The dog was saved, and much more.

What then? Did his tayle really wag? Ah, not so fast—remember Aesop's fox! If it was the inspired author's intention to write an historical description, then the answer is most certainly: Yes. But if the tail is no more than a vibrant instrument in the author's hand to give movement and life to a description of joyous homecoming, why then, it is possible that the dog is a literary ghost as the swine in the parable of the Prodigal Son are but parabolic or literary swine. Notice very carefully that this is a question of the author's historical *intention*, not of the author's historical *accuracy*. This is important. Catholic doctrine maintains that, granted the strictly historical intention, the accuracy is guaranteed by reason of Inspiration.

We have now raised the question of literary form in respect of a tiny passage in the book of Tobias. This momentous matter is more spectacularly urged, and not only in non-Catholic circles, in regard of a whole inspired book: a small book, indeed, of only four chapters but a book of great weight as we shall see; the book of Jonas. We introduce the topic because it is a popular one but much more because it admirably illustrates the issues involved in the "literary forms" principle.

The question is open to discussion. The authority of the Church has certainly not intervened with a specific pronouncement, nor perhaps is such a pronouncement probable, upon the intention of the inspired author of "Jonas". It is nevertheless important to remember the general directive of the Biblical Commission (in 1905; DB 1980). If an inspired book, says the decree, is commonly reckoned as historical, solid arguments must be forthcoming if one is to show that such was not in fact the author's mind. It follows that those loyal Catholic scholars who suspect a parabolical intention must, and do, seek to furnish these "solid arguments". So, for example, Richard Simon (who died in 1712), Gigot (1906), van Hoonacker (1908), Tobac (1921), Dennefeld (1924), Feuillet (1947). Many other equally responsible Catholic exegetes doubt the cogency of their arguments. But before we review the reasons for and against let us be clear that the doctrine of Inspiration is not infringed.

Does a discussion of the literary form of "Jonas" compromise the doctrine of Inspiration? It does not. Inspiration does not demand historical form. That our

Lord's parables, for instance, are committed to inspired writing does not turn them into histories. Literary form is not *in itself*—I do not speak of the literary form of this or that individual book—a matter of faith or of morals. Hence a careful theologian like van Noort can write: "With the proviso that the Church's decision is final in all matters of faith and morals, the identification of [biblical] literary forms is the business of literary criticism" ("Salvo iudicio ecclesiae in omnibus quae ad fidem moresque pertinent, determinatio speciei litterariae spectat ad artem criticam". *De Fontibus*, p. 53.) This question is of such moment that one or two more authorities should be mentioned. Thus van Hoonacker also warns us against a confusion, in this matter, between dogmatic tradition, which is binding and merely literary tradition which is not (*Les Douze Petits Prophètes*, p. 325). Sebastian Tromp, S. J. (*De Inspiratione*, p. 87) remarks: "Patristic tradition is binding [in this matter of literary forms] *if* dogmatic consequences are involved". Condamin, S.J. (*Dictionnaire Apologétique de la Foi Catholique*, col. 1556) and M.-J. Lagrange, O.P. (*Revue Biblique*, 1906, p. 153) write in the same sense. To these observations it should however be added that the Church alone is competent to decide if and when the literary form of a particular book does involve a matter of faith. Otherwise she is not the adequate custodian of the deposit of faith and of the sacred books.

We have mentioned Patristic tradition which, heir to the Jewish tradition on this subject, constitutes a powerful argument for the historical character of "Jonas". It is not that the Fathers were by any means ignorant of the difficulties—the old Whale argument at least already wearied, though it did not impress them. Poor Augustine in the fifth century was already tired of it. "I observe", he remarked, "that this business of Jonas tickles the pagans immensely" (*Patres Latini*, xxxiii. 382: "multo cachinno a paganis graviter irrisum animadverti"). His contem- porary, the forceful Jerome, was not amused either. In answer he rammed their own pagan legends down the jokers' throats: "What about Daphne being changed into a laurel? Or Jupiter, their supreme god, into a swan?" (*P.L.* xxv. 1132). These two, with the great majority of their fellow Fathers, plainly assume the historical charac- ter of the book. They assume it but it does not appear that they assert, still less impose, it—despite the fact that Jerome is fully aware of the controversies (*P.L.* xxv. 1117). One other warning should be signalled: Jerome thought highly of the Scriptural acumen of Gregory Nazianzen, somewhat his senior in years; now Gregory seems rather to have favoured the view that the book was, at least in part, an allegory and not a history. We had better have his own words; they are translated from the *Patres Graeci*, xxxv. 505–508:

I myself have spoken with one not unversed in these matters; he offered an explanation, far from absurd, of the seeming absurdities of the story. He is a man fully competent to sound the depths of the prophet.

Gregory follows up with an allegorical explanation of the "sea" which becomes "an ocean of sorrow". Unfor- tunately he breaks off here, promising "if God wills" to finish later. Did he? There are indications that he did and that the Fish himself became an allegory of Israel's fall. This, at least, is the probable conclusion from the fact that Theophylact in the twelfth century, commenting on "Jonas", uses practically the identical words used by Gregory and then goes on to develop fully the allegorical interpretation. It is hard to avoid the impression that he knew a later and more complete commentary of the same

Father. Now if "Gregory the Theologian" could speak like this, it would appear rash to insist that the historical character of the book of Jonas was regarded in his time as a matter of faith. In considering this problem, therefore, it would be wise to abstain from adducing "the unanimous consent of the Fathers" as a *dogmatic* argument though their general assumption of historical character holds its place, a strong place, in the line of literary tradition.

Having now cleared a part, but not all, of the ground shall we glance at the book itself? The story of Jonas is presented in four tableaux which correspond exactly to our four chapters of the book.

Scene One: Jonas in the Storm. Jonas has booked his passage Gibraltar-wards, that is to say to Tarshish, as far west as he and the Hebrews knew. He should really be on a camel bound for pagan Nineveh over the eastern desert but he is disobeying the voice of God. The author is telling us that Jonas is being as stubborn as he possibly could be and, whether it is fact or figure, he could not have done it better. Then comes the storm, described in terms reminiscent of Ezechiel (cf. Ezech. chapter xxvii; Ps. cvi, 23–32). The cargo is thrown overboard; the crew go down on their knees; Jonas is in the hold, fast asleep. It is bitterly ironical that pagans should pray while Yahweh's own prophet sleeps. The irony will appear again later when we find the great pagan city converted at a sentence from one prophet although Israel with the many words of many prophets had remained stubborn. Here it is the pagan crew that is converted and, when Jonas has been cast into the sea, the sailors "fear Yahweh exceedingly and sacrifice victims to Yahweh". This appears to be the climax of the chapter. It is a foretaste, too, of what is going to happen in Nineveh.

Scene Two: Jonas in the Fish. This chapter is almost wholly taken up with the famous canticle which reminds us so strongly of the accents of the book of Psalms. Considering the situation in which Jonas finds himself the note of thanksgiving may seem premature; this, however, may be possibly explained by the fact that he is safe at least so far, or else by the firmness of his hope in God's final deliverance. In any case the song is justified by the event and Jonas is again on "dry land"—where that dry land was we are not told.

Scene Three: Jonas in the City. "Jonas arose and went to Nineveh." He is obedient at last. But the inspired author does not think it necessary to describe the prophet's route; nor does he tell us the name of "the king of Nineveh" who joins his subjects in repentance. This conversion is a notable triumph for Israel's religion. Nineveh, centre and symbol of the power of Assyria (that enemy *par excellence* of Yahwism) is converted at the threat of a Hebrew prophet. A triumph certainly but perhaps a reproach too—an implied reproach for the obstinacy of the Chosen People.

Scene Four: Jonas in the Sulks. "Forty days and Nineveh will be destroyed", Jonas had said. He had spoken at God's command. But the heart of God was moved by the penance of Nineveh and the city was spared. Jonas was furious. He had feared all along, he said, that God was too easily swayed by a little repentance. He was disgusted; he wanted to die. He sat down outside the city still faintly hoping for the catastrophe he had promised. It does not make an attractive picture—the petulance of a child joined with the cold, selfish malice of a grown man. He would have the great city annihilated for the benefit of his prophetic reputation. It is surely not Jonas who is the hero of this book; the hero is God and the last word of the book is God's: "Shall I not spare?" The reader is left contemplating the hideous, or beautiful, irony of Man pleading the cause of vengeance while God meekly excuses himself for having pardoned the sinner. This is the satirical sting of the book of Jonas, and the sting is in the tail.

Now we are in a position to appreciate, at least in part, the two opposed views on the book. Both agree upon the high moral lesson it affords us and afforded its first readers; both agree (we speak for Catholic scholars) that the book is inspired and therefore without error; they differ only on the nature of the vehicle chosen by the author to convey his moral lesson. Does he narrate a *history* with a moral or does he compose a *story* with a moral? Is the book a history or a parable?

Before we go further, let us be fair to the parabolist. He is not scarified into his theory (again I speak for the Catholic exegete) by the *miracle* of the Fish. Even anti-miraculists do not find the Fish episode inconceivable— much less the Catholic. The huge sperm whale, which can scale 150 tons, I am told, is not a stranger even in the Mediterranean and one such has been found with a ten-foot shark inside him. As for the speed of the animal, it is only at first sight that this presents a problem. Fifteen knots, they say, is good for a whale. Now Jaffa is about four thousand miles from Nineveh, provided our Fish could thrash through the waterways of the Nile Delta into the Gulf of Suez. Allowing him the full seventy-two hours, such a journey would promote the beast to a prodigious pace of fifty knots. Incredible! Yes perhaps, but who said that the terminus was Nineveh? Certainly not the inspired text which speaks only of the "dry land". This reticence, we may observe, also serves to show how idle it is to ask: How did the Fish know whither Jonas was bound? We must not create difficulties by putting words into the author's mouth. In short, we might well hesitate to rule out the incident even on purely scientific grounds. But indeed these discussions are unnecessary where the omnipotence of God is to be reckoned with, and the parabolist is well aware of the fact. The Fish does play its part, though a secondary part only, in forming his decision but this is not because he considers the Fish impossible. The Fish is not impossible but, he thinks, the Fish episode is grotesque; it lends a touch of fantasy to the book. He maintains that this touch, taken with the reappearance of fantasy in other parts of the narrative, betrays the deliberate intention of the inspired author. He claims that the fantastic is characteristic of non-historical form and that the author expects the reader to recognize it as such.

We come at last to the arguments. The historicist and the parabolist each approaches the problem from his own distinctive angle. The parabolist claims the evidence of the text itself, intrinsic evidence; the historicist lays the emphasis rather upon extrinsic considerations (the majority opinion of Jewish and Christian interpreters, for instance). Each school, if it is to hold its own, must of course answer the objections of its fellow sincerely and adequately: the parabolist must not despise the external arguments nor the historicist the internal. One cannot take the offensive on one front without at least holding one's lines intact on the other. Thus when the historicist calls the witness of the book of Tobias the parabolist retorts that the alleged reading is far from sure; and in fact two of the three great manuscripts of the Greek Old Testament version contain it but the third reads otherwise and the Syriac, with our Vulgate (hence Douay), omits it altogether (" . . . because I know what Jonas the prophet has said concerning Nineveh: that it shall be destroyed". Tob. xiv. 4 in the Greek MSS. A & B; cf. Tob. xiv. 6 in Douay). On the other hand, when the parabolist seeks to turn this weapon of external evidence against his opponent the historicist has his riposte. The first objects that the conversion of

Nineveh is mentioned in no Assyrian document, the other answers that this is not surprising in view of the gaps in our Assyrian documentation. And so it goes on. All very discouraging.

Yet there is one argument which threatens the parabolic theory with the *coup de grâce*. It is built upon the words of the Truth himself whose knowledge was without limit (DB 2185). To the Pharisees our Lord retorted:

. . . A sign shall not be given it, except the sign of Jonah the prophet. For as "Jonah was in the belly of the whale three days and three nights", even so shall the Son of Man be in the heart of the earth three days and three nights. The men of Nineveh shall rise up at the judgment with this generation and shall condemn it: for they repented at the preaching of Jonah. (Matt. xii. 39–42, Westminster Version.)

The argument runs that our Lord would scarcely appeal to a fiction as a type of the fact of his own Resurrection; that still less could he reproach the Jews with an example of pagan conversion which in fact never took place. This second, very powerful, objection is reinforced by the sentence which follows our quotation:

The queen of the South shall rise at the judgment with this generation. (Matt. xii. 42.)

The Sheban queen was no merely parabolic figure and yet she stands side by side with the repentant Ninevites. This suggests, surely, that the conversion of Nineveh was equally an historical fact. At the least, says the historicist very justly, if we take Christ's words at their face-value there is not the slightest hint that the book of Jonas is no more than a parable. In reply the parabolist concedes that this is the most telling argument of all in favour of the historical interpretation. What has he to say? He claims that our

Lord's threat loses none of its force in the hypothesis of parable; he claims that if parable was sufficient for our Lord's purpose, then he who came to save and not to decide questions of literary criticism might well use as parable what some may have taken for history, and this without making any comment on his procedure. That parable *was* sufficient for our Lord's purpose, goes on the answer, is evident from the common conventions of language. Thus the great ghost of Nineveh may be said to "rise" in condemnation of Israel just as the thin vision of Banquo's offspring "rose" against Macbeth to his dismay. It may "rise" as "rose" the spectres of the slain "with twenty mortal murders on their crowns" to his dethroning. The parabolist argues that in this sense the great Shadow Figures of the parables could be said to rise in judgment against us: Samaritan, Publican, Prodigal in witness of our selfishness, pride, obstinacy. Such devices of language do not endow the shadow with substance; the ghost is sufficient for the speaker's purpose. St. Paul who for his own purpose borrows the magicians Jannes and Mambres from a Jewish apocryphal work does not *ipso facto* guarantee their historical existence under those names (2 Tim. iii. 8; cf. Spicq, *Les Épitres Pastorales*, 1947, p. 370f.; van Hoonacker, *Les Douze Petits Prophètes*, p. 323). Even our Lord himself, it is claimed, elsewhere condescends to use popular beliefs without pronouncing upon their objective value, a value which does not affect his argument (Matt. xii. 43–45; xvi. 1–4). As for the juxtaposition of the historical queen of Sheba and the parabolic repentant Ninevites, the parabolist will reply that one who preaches repentance may similarly juxtapose the Prodigal Son of the parable and the Magdalen of history. Nor does he find it unfitting that our Lord should use a literary figment as a type (not, of course, a proof) of his Resurrection. He reminds us that to call a man "a second Shylock", for example, does not commit one to the physical existence of the first; that when the priest prays: "Cleanse my lips as thou didst cleanse those of the prophet Isaias with a burning coal" he does not assert that the vision of Isaias (Isa. vi. 6f.) was more than vision; that the fact that Lazarus was only a figure in a parable does not force the Church to erase from her funeral service the words: "That with Lazarus who was once poor thou mayest have eternal rest". Such, at some length, is the answer of the parabolist. Some will think it adequate, others will not.

The intrinsic arguments, that is to say the indications sought in the book's own content, are used more eagerly in the parabolist school, though they are not the monopoly of either contending party. Those who favour the historical view note that the first contacts of Israel with Assyria did in fact take place in the eighth century—in the lifetime of the historical prophet whose name was Jonas (2 Kings xiv. 23); that historical sources assure us that Nineveh was indeed a huge city and a wicked one; that the quaint, apparently fantastic, practice of clothing cattle in the sackcloth of penance (Jonas. iii 8) was not unknown in the Persian empire at least; that the complex temperament of Jonas himself must have been drawn from life. Those who hold for parable willingly concede that the general *mise en scène* of the book—the relations of Israel and Assyria, the size and corruption of Nineveh— has verisimilitude, but they add, not unfairly, that this verisimilitude of background does not necessarily prove the inspired author's intention of writing good history; it is equally consistent with a desire to compose a good parable. The background, they say, proves nothing; they prefer to call our attention to a contempt for detail which would be strange in an historical account but which is a well-known phenomenon of parable. Thus in Scene Two the "dry land" is as vague as the "far country" where the Younger Son in the parable squandered his money and starved (Luke xv. 13); similarly in Scene Four the author seems to have no personal interest in Jonas whom he leaves, silenced by the divine voice, in the suburbs of Nineveh far from home; to this the parabolist compares the situation of the Elder Son in the parable of the Prodigal (Luke xv. 25–32) whose function is exhausted once he has provoked his father's reply. Nor, to pursue the argument, does Scene Three tell us how Jonas ultimately reached Nineveh—as the parable does not tell us how the Prodigal got home from the "far country". As for the anonymity of the "king of Nineveh", this may be due simply to the fact that, in the hypothesis of history, his name was unknown to the inspired historian; but the parabolist prefers again to see a studied vagueness reminding him of parable-phrases such as: a *certain* man had two sons, a *certain* man went into a far country, a *certain* man went down from Jerusalem to Jericho—and it is quite true that names are less important in parable than in history.

On the positive side the parabolist appeals to the artificial character of the whole work. The art reveals itself in many ways but most clearly, it is said, in the use made of other Old Testament books—Jeremias, Ezechiel, the Psalms. (The argument is developed and presented at its best by Father A. Feuillet in *Revue Biblique*, 1947, pp. 161–186.) The canticle in the second chapter does indeed suggest a harmony of echoes from the book of Psalms, for example. This argument, however, is not decisive. Granted the literary borrowings from books subsequent to the time of the prophet Jonas (eighth century), the immediate inference appears to be only that we owe our present form of Jonas's story to a later, inspired, writer; that the story may still be in fact a true history but a history used as a lesson for the sacred author's contemporaries and, for their pleasure and instruction, adorned with flowers of sacred literature. So, for instance, the canticle would not be the very words of Jonas himself but the inspired author's interpretation, in conventional Psalm-language, of his sentiments. In other words, this literary argument seems to lead us only to the conclusion that the story of Jonas has been used with great art and (as we shall see in the following essay) to great and topical purpose. It tells us that the inspired author was a writer of genius; it does not tell us whether he was a writer of religious fiction or an historian.

And there the matter rests, if indeed it may be said to rest when there are so many minds restlessly pursuing it. One can only appeal for patience. There are some things, even things bearing somewhat on the Faith, that must wait their turn. This patience is itself an exercise of Faith. Nevertheless, those whose duty it is to study these questions must labour to solve them even though, in God's will, they may never be solved this side of Heaven. The burden lies heavy on the conscience of the Catholic exegete in particular; it cannot be laid aside. The Holy Father in his recent encyclical, *Divino Afflante* (1943), after speaking of the difficulties in interpretation encountered by the Fathers and after praising the progress made "in the last few decades", especially in investigating and identifying literary forms, proceeds with these grave words:

If the Catholic exegete is to meet fully the requirements of modern biblical study he must, in expounding Sacred Scripture and vindicating its immunity from all error, make prudent use also of this further aid: he must, that is, ask himself how far the form of expression or literary idiom employed by the sacred writer may contribute to the true and genuine interpretation; and he may be sure that this part of his task cannot be neglected without great detriment to Catholic exegesis. (Encyclical *Divino Afflante;* C.T.S. trans., paragraph 42.)

VII

THE LESSON OF THE BOOK OF JONAS

Player Queen: None wed the second but who kill'd the first.
Hamlet [aside]: Wormwood, wormwood.

YOU REMEMBER how Hamlet pricked his stepfather to
self-betrayal by having the players perform *The Murder of
Gonzago*. To sharpen the edge of this thrust the Prince
himself subscribed some dozen lines more pointed than
the rest. Which were they? It would be foolish for an
amateur to raise his voice in the controversy but he may be
permitted a whispered guess. Is Hamlet's bitter "Wormwood" self-applause? It sounds a little like it. If so, the
queen's line is from his quill. But in any case Hamlet's
remark is scarcely necessary. Shakespeare's audience has
already been taken into the Ghost's confidence. Knowing
the real facts the audience keeps its eye on the guilty
Claudius and his consort to see how they are taking
it. The Player King and his Queen are heard but
not seen; as persons they are not important; they
are edged tools. Their lines, whether Hamlet under-
scores them or not, contain an ironical significance;
otherwise their play-within-play is cheap melodrama,
no more.

We make these few remarks to indicate the importance
of knowing the background, historical or social or religious
and so on, of any delicate literary work. Especially is
this knowledge vital for the understanding of satirical

literature, like *Gulliver's Travels* for instance. If we are ignorant of the background we miss the irony; if we miss the irony we miss the point.

Now the author of the book of Jonas never cries "Wormwood", even when the worm eats the wood of Jonas's ivy in the satirical Scene Four (iv. 7). Still, he is certainly muttering it to himself as he writes. And we shall have to give him our close attention because he is not a simple man. His book is a laborious, though not laboured, piece of craftsmanship. The work is woven of threads from his inspired predecessors, from Jeremias especially, and the pattern is symmetrical.

When the curtain rises on the first Act, Jonas is discovered receiving his mission from God. Enter then the pagan sailors and this scene ends with their conversion. The Act closes with Jonas's prayer to God. The opening of the second Act repeats that of the first; it is followed by the entrance of the pagan Ninevites who, like the sailors, are converted. This Act, too, closes with Jonas's prayer. Whether the book be history or parable, it is certain that the inspired author has arranged his material, fact or fancy, with a purpose. What is this purpose?

The solution we propose is offered by Fr. Feuillet (*Revue Biblique*, 1947, 340–361); it is neighbour to that outlined by S. R. Driver (*Introduction to the Literature of the O.T.*, 1891, 323f.) and to that of the Catholic exegete of Louvain, Canon van Hoonacker (*Les Douze Petits Prophètes*, 1908, 312–325). Unlike other interpretations it does not mangle the book. In this it favourably contrasts with the solutions of many of the critics, each shuffling the texts in his own way like a pack of cards (cf. Bewer, *International Critical Commentary*, *Jonah*, 1912, 13–21). Moreover, it has the advantage even over van Hoonacker's exposition by preserving the unity of the book's fundamental lesson.

After all the excitement of the Storm- and the Fish-episodes the reader has the impression that he, with Jonas, is back at the starting-point. The author conveys this impression by coldly repeating the original divine command: "Go to Nineveh and there preach!" (iii. 2; cf. i. 2). A sort of *"Now* will you do what you are told?" but spoken with the calm persistence of God. To what end, then, all this elaborate account of escape and recapture? To demonstrate the essential truth that God has a strong hold on Jonas; that Jonas is truly God's prophet and, consequently, that his message is truly God's. We shall see the importance of this point later. But the flight of Jonas is an attempt to shirk his God-given mission or, at least, the author's device by which he paints such a withdrawal. For it should be noticed, in passing, that the flight wears the air of literary artifice: a prophet fully persuaded of God's ubiquity (cf. i. 9) could hardly hope to escape the Omnipresent. But whether real flight or no, the Fish is God's net thrown wide to capture him. The Fish is God's agent who arrests Jonas and drags him back to his duty. But the Fish has a further significance: it gives Jonas the appearance of a true prophet. Whether God himself or the inspired author created the animal, it has the effect of putting Jonas on a level with Elias, who had his ravens, and with Eliseus who was vindicated by bears, and with the soothsayer Balaam who, for once a true prophet, was carried to his prophetic task against his will on the back of his marvellous ass. The Fish, therefore, is not only a sharp remembrancer of duty; it is a privilege also; it is God's vehicle for his prophet. This explains the thanksgiving note of the canticle (chapter ii) which, at first hearing, seems so discordant and which has led many a critic to dub the song an "insertion" or a "transposition". As for the form of the canticle, a jigsaw of texts from the psalmist-prophets, this too invites us to recognize the genuine voice of prophecy in Jonas's mouth. In short, we are assured of one thing when we have reached the middle of the book, namely that Jonas, whoever he is, is a prophet of God and that his message, whatever happens to it, is God's message.

But why should the author be at such pains to drive this lesson home? Why use fifty per cent of his space to do so? Because, presumably, he considered it important, indispensable to his purpose. Paradoxically enough, Jonas had to be proved a true prophet precisely because his prediction was to prove false. We are not just playing with words. Observe now: "Nineveh shall be destroyed"— *and Nineveh was not destroyed.* The prediction was God-sent and the prediction was falsified—*falsified by repentance, Man's and God's.* We must pause here. We stand before the great lesson of Jonas.

When the book of Jonas was being written, probably in the fifth century, after the Exile, impatient Israel was expecting the messianic age of prosperity. "Where is the God of judgment?" it cried (Mal. ii. 17). Its prophets had fulminated messages of destruction against Tyre and Babylon and the rest (e.g. Ezech. xxvi–xxviii; Isa. xlvii), yet Tyre had not been destroyed and Babylon still stood. What, then? Were the prophets false prophets? Surely if the prophet "foretelleth and it cometh not to pass, that thing the Lord hath not spoken"? (Deut. xviii. 21–22). Now it is precisely that very topical problem which takes definite shape in the book of Jonas—Jonas who has been elaborately introduced as a genuine, God-sent, prophet; Jonas whose prediction, nevertheless, is to remain unfulfilled. But if the book of Jonas propounds the problem it also puts us on the path to its solution, though to read him aright we shall have to borrow spectacles which he, in his turn, had borrowed from Jeremias. For indeed, we might parenthetically observe, the Hebrew phrases and the theological ideas which Jonas uses show a profound indebtedness to Jeremias. If such procedure seem surprising we must be reminded that it was not unusual among the inspired writers, especially after the Exile. Isaias, for instance, borrows from Amos, Jeremias from Osee, Ezechiel from Jeremias.

How does Jeremias help us here? By giving precision to the sentence of Deuteronomy we have just quoted. (May we recall that the revelation of the Old Testament is a growing thing; it develops?) The optimistic prophet, says Jeremias characteristically, is to be suspected. Why? Because he may be currying favour. In fact he often was—King Achab had four hundred such sycophantic "prophets" (3 Kings xxii. 6). The justification of the prophet must wait upon the event. But for the prophets of destruction Jeremias lays down no such condition. Odd? No, because—for Jeremias—prophecies of destruction are really invitations to repentance and such invitations must be of God. Such threats are therefore conditional:

If that nation against which I have spoken *shall repent of their evil, I also will repent of the evil that I have thought to do to them* (Jer. xviii. 8).

This idea of God "reversing" his heavy sentence is not strange to the Old Testament (eg. Exod. xxxii. 14; Judges ii. 18; 2 Kings xxiv. 16; Amos vii. 3)—more than once "the Lord was appeased from doing the evil which he had spoken against his people". But it is Jeremias the "prophet of the nations" (Jer. i. 5) who sees that the Gentiles also may hope for this beautiful "repentance" of God. The book of Jonas joins its voice with his. "Gentiles?" it says, "aye, even Nineveh, that type of all wickedness!" The book says this. But Jonas himself? Ah, he has not learned the lesson yet.

In the Storm, Fish and City scenes we saw Jonas the prophet; in the fourth and last ("the Sulks") we see Jonas the man. And not a lovable man either—the only unlikeable character in the book. In what elegant terms he praised the mercy of God when he was the object of it (Canticle; Scene Two)! How bitterly he deplores that same mercy when it visits Nineveh (iv. 2, cf. ii. 2)! How he bewailed the loss of his own ivy-shelter, but how he longed for the collapse of a thousand roofs in pagan Nineveh! Can anyone miss the satire here? That God reads him his lesson so gently only makes the satire more telling. The author is not going to spoil everything by underlining it. He leaves it to our wits. One thing is certain: the author does not want us to admire this Jonas of Scene Four. If Jonas is a real, live prophet we are assisting at his education; he is not yet the finished article. Whether real or not, he is the mouthpiece—or personification—of narrow and malignant nationalism, an attitude not uncommon in Israel particularly after the Exile. This attitude the author holds up to ridicule. How dismayed he would be to think we could have a vague admiration for Jonas! In this last chapter Jonas is the villain of the piece. He is the contemporary nationalist spirit howling for its foes' destruction, expecting it as a divinely-promised right, failing—if we may use Christian terms—to love the sinner while hating the sin. A shocking attitude? Yes indeed; but who throws the first stone? Some of us can remember the "scandal" of many when a certain notorious film-star died in the peace of the Church. Yet we had not the evidence the Jews had against Nineveh!

And, after all, was righteous Israel itself so sinless? Israel, deaf to prophet after prophet and blind to her own deafness? (cf. 2 Esdras ix. 26; Mal. ii. 17). Here we meet yet another lesson of this amazing book. In its own ironical fashion it bids Israel turn her own eyes inwards. Is God's nation so much more worthy than its enemies? it asks. It answers with one grand, condemnatory "If" that rings strangely like the sentence of our Lord:

If in Tyre and Sidon had been wrought the miracles that have been wrought in you, they had long ago done penance (Matt. xi. 21).

The book of Jonas hangs the painted canvas of satirical caricature as a backcloth to the solemn hypocrisy of Israel. In the foreground stands the faithless City of God, the Jerusalem that stoned the prophets. Behind it, in monstrous contrast, our author shows us Devil's Town changing its wicked heart at one word from one prophet, and him a stranger. If—perhaps we should say "even if"—the background is only two-dimensional, lacking the solidity of historical fact, it cannot take the tooth out of the biting satire. Would that the Jews had learned from it! But the warning of the book of Jonas became a prophecy and there came a Prophet who was without a hearing in his own country. "If in Tyre and Sidon. . . ." he said, and "Jerusalem, Jerusalem . . . thou wouldst not". The "sign of Jonas" indeed!

It is not the least of the paradoxes of the Old Testament that its religion is at once universal and national. One only God had chosen one single nation. We who have attributed to guardian angels the strain "Rule Britannia!" can scarcely be shocked if a human nation so privileged should lose its balance.

In certain circles of fifth century Judaism, therefore, we find a ferocious and haughty nationalism which sorts ill with the genuine message of the prophets. This attitude issues from the consciousness of being a Chosen People. It is a child of that consciousness, but an illegitimate child. The attitude can be explained; it cannot be excused. Nevertheless a certain exclusiveness was necessary because purity of race safeguarded purity of religion. I mean, necessary in practice and at that time. Hence the contemporary laws against foreign marriages were an admirable exercise of religious prudence (1 Esdras ix. 12; 2 Esdras xiii. 1–3). As such they were backed by the prophet Malachy (ii. 10–12). But there was no lack of balance here: official Judaism welcomed pagan converts (2 Esdras x. 28f.). Malachy himself looked forward to the time when true sacrifice would not be the monopoly of Judaism but would be offered by Gentiles, too, from lands of the rising sun to the places of its setting. The paradox of a religion universal but national was already being resolved. This paradox, like every other, was contradiction in appearance only. The religion of Israel was in principle universal, in practice—and only for a time—national. Malachy for example, fully appreciated this point. Less religious and less instructed circles did not. It was inconceivable for them that Israel could ever sink its individuality in one great family of God. Against this mentality, which is represented by the figure of Jonas himself, the book of Jonas barbs its shafts.

There is a phrase, not rarely repeated: "the terrible God of the Hebrews". To it the book of Jonas is the great retort. It is the voice of God's pity for all his creation: Nineveh, even Nineveh that wicked city, is God's beloved. With grief he had watched it grow in sin, but he could never bring himself to punish. This fatal weakness of his, as Jonas himself might have called it, prevented him. He was, as Jonas said with impertinent and savage complaint, a God too "gentle, sympathetic, not easily stirred to anger, prodigal of his goodness, lightly forgiving". You and I, of the Gentiles, may thank God and his inspired author for that complaint. We may thank him, too, that he has not given the last word to Jonas. He has given it, as always, to his own divine pity. The book ends with God's (God's!) plea against hard human justice: "Shall I not spare?"

VIII

THE CRAFTY EXEGETE AND THE BEGINNING OF GENESIS

When the Church could no longer deny the facts that scholars put forward, it contrived to retain its power by smilingly adopting science and learning with an air of: " Of course we know all that, and it makes no difference to the truth of Christianity." Symbolism and allegory were again helpful to the Church. (MARJORIE BOWEN, *The Church and Social Progress*, Thinkers' Library, p. 82.)

IT WAS shortly after writing the pages on the Canticle-allegory and the Jonas-parable that I took a holiday, at peace with all the world. But in this warring vale we cry: Peace, peace—and there is no peace. I met Miss Bowen, though not in person, on the Yorkshire coast. My conscience was stirred. There stood I in the bookshop, my hands still red with "symbolism and allegory". One who, a few days before, had smilingly adopted "science and learning"—and not less the villain for smiling. And here was the voice of the Thinkers' Library, no less, denouncing me to the world as "that smooth-faced gentleman, tickling Commodity". Now, since we have to do with the Thinkers' Library, we cannot dispense ourselves from earnest thought. We must roll up our sleeves. But, before we begin, may we make one little point clear? The term "Church" coming from a non-Catholic nib —I do not use the word in a colloquial sense—is a wide one. We can undertake to explain the attitude only of that "Church" whose servant we have the honour to be.

Nothing, it seems, will ever dispel the impression that all

her difficulties have rushed upon the Church since the Renaissance. That is to say, presumably, since men first began to think for themselves. Things must have been dreadful before the advent of "science and learning". But men did have their difficulties, you know. It is just about seventeen hundred years since Origen put his foot down in the name of commonsense:

What rational creature would be prepared to believe there was a first, second and third day, morning and evening, before the sun was made? (*De Principiis.* IV. 3).

You see? The difficulties against the Creation account may be good difficulties but they are certainly not new difficulties. Even third century science could not stomach this.

Two hundred years later, Augustine was losing patience with the good old objections:

What do I care if the heavens are a circumambient sphere and not a sort of dishcover? (*PL.* XXXIV. 270).

In the thirteenth century they were still at it. All up-to-date astrologers now knew that some stars at least were bigger than the moon. It fell now to Aquinas to answer the obvious objection drawn from the "lesser lights" that Genesis speaks about. He does so in his usual cool way—he was ice compared with Origen and Augustine:

Some stars may be bigger than the moon, but the moon means more to us down here; moreover, it looks bigger (*Summa Theologica*, 1, 70, 1 ad 5m).

Clearly this "smiling adoption" business was early in vogue. But how did Aquinas and Augustine and Origen justify themselves? All three, without the slightest doubt, believed in the omniscient and inspiring Spirit. How exempt him from error? None of them seemed to feel any anxiety. Origen, lecturing at Alexandria, was a great allegorist. He certainly did not deny the objective truth of the fact of Creation (see the Preface of his *De Principiis*) but he appealed to a "higher sense", refusing to believe that the Spirit would be bothered with scientific teaching. Augustine followed much the same line:

When people come along with arguments like this, tell them that the Spirit had no intention of teaching things useless to salvation (*PL.* XXXIV. 270).

St. Thomas Aquinas, less curt than Augustine in this, spread himself a little on the subject. He explained that the book of Genesis was addressed to simple folk. For this reason, for example, it did not mention the creation of Air because what the eye does not see the simple heart does not grieve over (cf. *Summa*, I, 68, 3 corp.).

Now has the Church changed any of these principles under the pressure of modern science? If she has, she may fairly be accused of opportunism and "smiling adoption" and the rest. But she did not change because, to take the meanest view of her, she did not need to change. Aquinas may have had more scientific objections to deal with than Augustine had, but he still used the same answer. He needed no other. In the twentieth century we are in the same case. There is not a new objection: it is an old one re-presented, though not reinforced, with new examples. Like Augustine we still see no reason why God should favour an inspired author with a scientific revelation. There is no evidence that science has brought man nearer to God in the twentieth century than its pitiful antecedent brought him in the first.

May we explain our position to our opponents? We do not claim that the inspired author of the first chapter of

Genesis knew more than his contemporaries about the scientific "how" of the world's becoming. Had you asked him what he meant by referring to the primal abyss of waters when he should have been describing a nebula, he would most certainly have gaped. "If what you call a nebula", we can hear him saying, "is as formless as my abyss of waters, go ahead, call it what you like. All I wanted to say was that God called order from chaos. Didn't you guess I was not writing a treatise on science?" Why, even people who know better are very free with their terms. A Moral Theologian who is not usually given to jesting (Noldin, S.J., *Theologia Moralis*, 2 : 677) can cheerfully write, speaking of the Friday abstinence: "Under the term fish we include reptiles and crustaceans." And what would a zoologist say to that? Let us keep our sense of proportion. Hear Thomasheen James:

T.J.: She has Patsy like a bird sittin' stupid on a bough an' the scorpion crawlin' up to him on a hunderd legs.
Sobersides: Your zoology is a bit mixed.
T.J.: What harm? The result is identic.

Where, then, is the Inspiration of the first chapter of Genesis, and where—if anywhere—is its Revelation? Let us say at once that all is *inspired* and only part, but this the important part, *revealed*. It is opportune to recall in this place what has been said before regarding this word "revealed". You will remember that, although all Scripture is "revelation" in the sense of "an authoritative communication by God to man", not all of it is revelation in the narrow sense of which we are speaking here. In this restricted sense "revelation" is the communication by God to man of a truth hitherto unknown.

Now it is important to distinguish the religious teaching of this chapter of Genesis from the framework in which it is presented. Both proceed from an *inspired* author but only the teaching is *revealed*. Here is something of the teaching: the universe did not itself struggle purposefully into ordered existence, as in the picturesque but pantheistic Babylonian account. Nor did the universe spontaneously but blindly evolve—though it so evolved according to the atheistic Phoenician record. On the contrary, it was brought into being (says Genesis) and from being into ordered existence by an intelligent Creator distinct from the universe he had made. The author has something to say about the heavenly bodies, too; something upon which we might reflect even in this great era of science when the newspaper will offer you your horoscope. The lights of heaven, he says, are there to mark the seasons, not, as for so many Semites, to be adored. As for Man, he is constituted above the rest of creation by reason of a divine act conferring a mysterious "likeness" to God. None of these topics, you will notice, is old-fashioned. Each is of abiding interest and each is beyond the reach of physical science. The author's source of information? Revelation, as we shall see.

So much for the substance. What of the framework? What, for instance, of the *order* in which the different creatures emerged? It is the order of the less to the more perfect, and this is a natural enough order for the unaided human mind to conceive. It is found roughly the same in the pagan accounts. If this order turns out to be in general accord with the findings of science, we shall not claim that it has been revealed. We shall ascribe the agreement to chance or, better, to the fact that human reason is a reflection of the divine intelligence. We believe, with Augustine, that the Spirit was not concerned to reveal information that had no relish of salvation in it. For that sort of information, true to the unchanged principle, we look to the scientist. And if ever in the heat of argument some of us have lost sight of the principle, we freely offer our apologies to the scientist and to the traditional doctrine of the Church which Augustine voiced so well. I am thinking, of course, of Galileo Galilei who is (though he lived and died a faithful son of the Church) a protégé of the Thinkers' Library. We shall not repeat the weary old arguments. We merely recall that the decrees of the famous Congregation (in 1616 and 1633) were disciplinary. The reason for the condemnation given by the members ("as being opposed to sacred Scripture", etc.) was erroneous but the reasons are not the formal object of the decree. It remains true, however, that the authors of the decree had failed to apply the old principle.

What of the "days" of Creation? Did the author think that the world as we see it took only six days to make? What does it matter? the time-element is as unimportant to salvation as the order of creation. We may reasonably assume that the author of this religious passage did not intend to commit himself to a formal scientific statement that had nothing to do with his purpose. For the same reason we may presume that he would have no revelation to guide him. What would he have? Either his own commonsense or the ideas of his contemporaries. To take the second first: what were these ideas? It is hard to discover, but the exciting events of the Babylonian myth could scarcely be crowded into one week. It has even been conjectured that the Babylonians allowed over one million and a half years for the process of "creation". Of course, creation does take longer when you have to fight with other gods. Genesis, with its one God, would get no help from that direction. What, then, of the author's unaided commonsense? What would this tell him? Well, knowing as he did that God created by a word, I should imagine that he thought the whole business instantaneous. Then why "days" at all—and very odd days, too, when there was no sun for the first three of them? Ah, why indeed; unless he wanted the number six. But why should he want six? His choice is clearly deliberate: the obvious number for him to choose was eight because he recounts eight distinct works. It is a personal choice, too: we do not find this number in the Babylonian or Phoenician accounts; the seven tablets on which the Babylonian story is written might appear to suggest the six days' work and one day's rest of Genesis, but in fact these seven tablets are not seven divisions of the creation-work properly so called; this does not begin until tablet four. We must therefore seek an explanation from Hebrew practice. It is there we find, deeply rooted, the six-day working week with the solemn injunction of the seventh day rest (Exod. xxiii. 12). It is reasonable, then, to suppose that the Hebrew author is using an extended anthropomorphism: God's great work is described *in terms of* man's weekly labour. It is further probable that he wishes to present man with a divine *model* for his work and rest, thus driving home the practice of the Sabbath.

There are popular writers who speak very glibly of the likeness between the pagan cosmogonies and the Genesis story. One sometimes wonders if they have ever read either. You see, the scholars are much more cautious, not to say antagonistic. Listen:

But there is no foundation whatsoever for the assertion which has so often been made that the two accounts of Creation which are given in the early chapters of Genesis are derived from the Seven Tablets of Creation described in the preceding pages. The fundamental conceptions of the Babylonian and Hebrew accounts are essentially different. (Wallis Budge, *The Babylonian Legends of the Creation*, ed. Sidney Smith, British Museum, 1931).

I should say they are! Having just laboured again through the wild and wearisome Seven Tablets I turn with relief to the profound simplicity of Genesis. To take just one example of surface similarity combined with deep distinction: it takes the god Marduk one hundred lines of epic to split "like a shell-fish" the hostile goddess who is Tiamat, one half of Chaos, and to push up the top part to form the heavens. Genesis is much less exciting: "And God said: Let there be a firmament made amidst the waters; and let it divide the waters from the waters. . . . And it was so." What if the biblical *Tehom*, the deep, has the same name as the chaotic Tiamat? The *name* is common to all the Semitic languages (cf. Deimel, *Verbum Domini*, 1923, p.159), it is the *thing* that matters. If people call the account of Genesis "myth", what word have they got left for the Tablets?

It is proved fact that the serene monotheism and effortless creation of Genesis stand alone in the Semitic world: witnesses have risen from the soil of Assyria to confirm it. This is not a hasty cry of triumph; it is the considered verdict of scholars. The words written fifty years ago by Lagrange (*Revue Biblique*, 1896, p. 403) need no revision in the light of subsequent discovery:

The idea of creation by a simple word was never the product of a Semitic mind . . . and since a transcendental effect demands a transcendental cause, *the most rational explanation of the Mosaic cosmogony is still Revelation.*

This may not make headlines in the sensational Press but it should provide thought for the Thinkers' Library.

IX

IN PRAISE OF MAN. A LESSON FROM GENESIS

WE CAN squander much valuable time and space on explaining what the sacred writers do not mean. It is true that we owe this duty to our unbelieving neighbours but we must not allow ourselves to lose sight of the plain and positive message of Holy Writ. What we have done for the book of Jonas, therefore, we shall do in part for the opening chapters of Genesis. We shall find, I promise you, that the old author has things to say about you and me vastly more sound than many of our modern prophets have to offer. For we do indeed need a tonic these days with Evolutionists reminding us of our simian beginnings and Revolutionists prescribing our slavish end. We have had enough of Monkeydom and Flunkeydom. Let us sit back and admire ourselves for a change! It is surely more important to know what we are than to guess what we were, at a time when we were not; than to conjecture what we shall be, in a future we may never see. It is precisely that important question which the two opening chapters of Genesis seek to answer. They are only indirectly concerned with the other two—a remark not without significance. And the answer? "Little less than the angels" (cf. Ps. viii. 6). An answer sure of a laugh in circles not otherwise conspicious for humility, but an answer which perhaps finds sympathy in the heart of the common man who feels that he is not so common after all.

Allegory and parable have recently passed before our notice. Now let us consider history and, for the present, what may be called Primal History. For there is a record of man's activities which derives from written documents, and this we may call history proper; and there is a record painfully gathered from dumb remains like bones and pottery, and this we may call anthropological history; and there is a record which lays claim to no documentary evidence at all. This last is Primal History and you find it in the first chapters of Genesis. It is history because it is an account of human incidents. But, in the absence of documentation of any kind, is it *true* history?

Now let us say at once that since the normal conditions of exact history are lacking—I mean the evidence, immediate or mediate, of those who saw the events flowing in life or who see their results frozen in the soil— we cannot establish the historical accuracy of the first two chapters of Genesis by the ordinary means. No man stood by when the universe was taking shape, nor was the first man a witness of his own making. In any case, our inspired story of Creation was not written until perhaps one hundred thousand years, which is a very conservative figure, after the appearance of the first man. On the other hand, it is quite clear that the author intends us to believe the facts that underlie his figures of speech. It is equally plain that he believes them himself. But what proof does he offer? None.

Let us be clear in our minds. The ultimate guarantee of the story is not historical evidence but *Revelation*. When was the revelation made? To the first man, surely. But after? What of its transmission through thousands of years down to our author? We know nothing. But we do know that whatever primitive revelation there may have been was eventually warped. We know that the ancestors of Abraham, progenitor of Israel, were idolaters (Josue xxiv.

2), whereas our story breathes the purest monotheism. It looks as if the revelation had to be renewed either to Abraham or to his decendants or to Moses himself. But it is always "revelation", you see. The Gospels can stand on their own feet but, without an infallible Church, we might say that the story of Creation is a noble story or even the most probable story yet we could still beg to doubt if it was the true story. That the Church has declared the dogma of Creation is evidence, though not immediately of the historical order, that the account of Genesis is neither myth, allegory nor false history. It is evidence that what the account teaches—not the figures of speech used—truly answers to what actually happened. The Modernist might airily say that the dogma dispenses with the historicity, but the Catholic holds that the dogma presupposes the historicity and, in passing, declares it. We shall leave the matter there for the present.

"Let there be Light!" cries a great Voice. For, as man thinks, what can be done without it? From the created, formless mass a cosmic stage is to be made and set. For whom? For Man, as you shall see. Light, then! And when that thin substance spreads itself for the second time ("*second* day") a giant work begins. I say "thin substance", for so, it seems, the author's contemporaries thought and so, it would appear, the author speaks (cf. the encyclical *Providentissimus Deus*, 1893; Denzinger-Bannwart, 1947). God not revealing, he knew no better. The work of this second day is like the reclaiming of submerged Atlantis or of Lyonesse. The waters of the covering ocean are sucked up to leave, below their containing firmament, a broad band of air and those waters only that are to serve the earth. On the *third* day, the emergence and draining of the lovely land with its grassy coat. The Stage is now there with its three compartments: Light, Air-Sea, Land.

Now, says our methodical author, for the furniture of each compartment in turn. Denizens of Light first: sun, moon, stars (*fourth* day). Wings now for the Air and fins for the Sea (*fifth* day). There is nothing yet on the green carpet but we feel that the earth is already pregnant with life: "Let the earth bring forth!" (*sixth* day). Out come the brutes, and not a man amongst them. We are right at the end of this six-day week now and the set Stage is expectant. Birds, fish, beasts are all there waiting for something. For what?

Now it is just here that the author is in difficulties. He is committed to a six-day working week and he has already given Friday (or Saturday in our arrangement of the week) to the production of the beasts. He cannot afford a separate day for Man and yet is determined to give him prominence. What to do? Now we have all felt that hesitant mood in which we take the chair, as it were, at a debate of two sides of our "self". It is a psychological trinity. Our bold and intelligent author seizes upon this experience to give that necessary sense of deliberate pause, as good as an extra day to him, which introduces a decision of moment: "Let *Us* make Man!" We might here be excused a brief digression on this pronoun "us" which has often proved troublesome. We have assumed that it is a "deliberative" plural because the majestic "We" is unknown in Hebrew (cf. Joüon, *Grammaire de l'Hébreu Biblique*, 114e). The clearly monotheistic character of the narrative resists the suggestion that we have here "a vestige of polytheism"; it would be a curious oversight on the part of the editor and the later our document (very late—fifth century—according to some critics) the more curious the oversight. The phrase is admirably explained in the light of the doctrine of the blessed Trinity but this is not the same as saying that the author was aware of this doctrine. Not a few of the Fathers (and cf. St. Thomas,

Summa, ii–ii, 174, 6) explicitly declare that this mystery was not revealed until New Testament times (cf. Lebreton, *Histoire du dogme de la Trinité*, p. 555).

"Let us make Man." By a sort of mass-production the Seas may be ordered to "swarm with" fish and the Land to "bring forth" beasts, but this will not do for Man. The last of the creatures demands the touch of the Master himself or, it is more accurate to say, his undivided attention. More accurate, because the account of the first chapter is very abstract indeed and the author refuses to stoop, or rise, to the audacious imagery of the second. Man is God's special work, that is all—and enough. Of the precise manner of his making the author says nothing; he must not be dragged into controversy on this point. He is concerned with Man as he knows him—a thing high above the beasts in origin but also, and chiefly, in nature. In image and in likeness, which is to say without and within, Man is in some sort a reflection of the God to whom the author has introduced us. This means that Man, too, in his measure, is wise, beneficent, strong lord of nature. The thought proves too much for our matter-of-fact writer and even he, unexpectedly enough, bursts into song:

> *And God created Man in his own* image!
> *To the image of* God *he created him!*
> *Male and female he created them!*

We feel like clapping our hands and shouting. There is no doubt that the author meant us to feel that way and I had rather his verse than a thousand pages of anthropology.

"Behold I have given you every herb . . . and all trees to be your food." I suppose that the inspired writer, being of a pastoral people, ate mutton without any sense of guilt. Yet he evidently considers it indelicate to strike this jarring note in his peaceful symphony. The concord of man and beast must be allowed to remain and preserve the atmosphere of idyll. There is no allusion, therefore, to Man the carnivore. It is probable that this silence is merely symbolic. When Isaias speaks of the returning Golden Age he, in the same vein, commits his lions to a diet of straw (Isa. xi. 7). One is inclined to think that the fruit and vegetable menu of Adam is not meant to be an exhaustive list. Many, however, maintain that the author of this chapter depicts the first man as a vegetarian (thus Chaine, for example; *Le Livre de la Genèse*, 1948, p. 29), wishing to inculcate a great respect for life, the gift of God. The problem is a little complex. We have seen that the first chapter of Genesis rather pointedly avoids mentioning animal-slaughter; but in the third chapter God clothes the fallen ones with the skins of animals. In the fourth chapter, too, Abel's animal-sacrifice is found pleasing to God, and chapter seven draws the distinction between "clean and unclean" animals who enter the Ark, a distinction which suggests the legal injunctions regarding food. Chapter nine, on the other hand, seems to hint at primitive vegetarianism: to Noe, after the Deluge, is given the first explicit permission of a meat-diet. To this difficulty it may be sufficient to answer, as we have suggested, that the first chapter contains not a complete menu but a symbol of peace only. In this case, the permission of meat in chapter nine may be no more a first permission than the mention of homicide in the same chapter (ix. 5) is the first prohibition of the same. Nevertheless many, including the Catholic exegete Heinisch, are not satisfied. These invoke the hypothesis of documents to explain the two different points of view. Chapters one and nine are assigned to the one document ("P") which supposes primitive vegetarianism, and chapters, three, four and seven to another document ("J") which does not. It should be remembered that the possibility of Moses' use of existing documents is expressly conceded by the Biblical Commission (Den-zinger-Bannwart 1999) and we have already seen (page 14) the compatibility of this course with the doctrine of Inspiration together with its effect upon interpretation.

The second account of Creation is more homely. I say the "second" account because it is fairly generally admitted, and not only in non-Catholic circles, that we have a second account in the second chapter of Genesis—the second document being grouped with the first by an inspired author (cf. Pirot, *Dictionnaire de la Bible, Supplément*, 1, 86; Hoepfl, O.S.B., *Dictionnaire Apologétique de la Foi Catholique*, 3, 1908). The Creative Voice of chapter one becomes the Potter of chapter two. He fashions the surface-earth to the shape of Man. Man, in Hebrew *adam*, is of the soil, *adamah*. Thus the author plays on words to suit his purpose which is not a lesson in etymology but a reminder to Man of his lowly origin on the material side. The actual derivation of the word *adam* is probably from the Assyrian root *udmu* meaning "human race". Into that shape, then, God breathes his own breath and with this breath Man becomes a living being. There and then and not before? We shall have to examine this question later but meanwhile it is of the utmost importance to remember that the graphic form of the story warns us against asking too much of the author. Certainly his lofty tone forbids us to imagine a God made in the likeness of Man. The "breath" no more implies lungs than the "flame from his nostrils" of the psalmist (Ps. xvii. 9) demands a nose. Human speech is, after all, a halting thing. In this respect even *our* withers are not unwrung; for us God is "he", not "she" or "it", yet we know he is not masculine but a Spirit. We speak of God's turning away from the sinner when it is the sinner turning away from God—and so forth. But still, metaphors are not idle. What is God's "breathing", then? The gift of life? No, not this only, because the beasts have life without this singular mention of the breath of God (Gen. ii.19). It is just this "breath" that gives Man his distinction. He has much in common with beasts. The ancient writer knew this better than we do: he had not the thick cosmetic of modern and western civilization to deceive him. But he did not lose his balance as some of our contemporaries lose it. He saw well enough the difference between the leprous beggar sitting on the village refuse-dump and the pariah dog that prowled about it. The "breath" is that immaterial thing of high origin which expresses, in more vivid form, the "image and likeness" of the first Creation account. True, the author does not assume the philosopher but, after all, has philosophy really got much further than this? It is no great progress to put "breath" into Latin and call it "spirit".

The periodical *John Bull* and the *Dictionnaire d'Archéologie Chrétienne* have little in common. It came therefore as a surprise, I confess, to read in this same *Dictionnaire* (5, 1350) the words: "H. Bottomley dans *John Bull*." The hairy old story of the Council of Mâcon had evidently come to Mr. Bottomley's ears: a Christian bishop had doubted whether women had a soul at all! Though it is somewhat off our point and, if we may say it without contempt, beneath our notice, may we be forgiven a brief comment now that we have raised the topic? The bishop's doubt at the Council (A.D. 585) was not expressed in the meetings but in private conversation. As for the doubt itself, it was purely terminological—whether the term "homo" could rightly be used of woman. We might remark, without rancour, that the diligence of those who seek out such hole-and-corner difficulties is rather suspicious: it seems to suggest a shortage of heavier ammunition. The Catholic Church seems to be a favourite target. So far as I know, the world has not yet raised its voice against the Jews, nor do I suggest it should, on the ground that the Talmud proclaims "the virgin who spends her time in prayer, the scourge of the world" But, I forget; perhaps the world agrees.

But let us leave our unfortunate bishop. Whatever we have to say about him there is no doubt about the sentiments of the author of Genesis chapter two. In his eyes woman is of one nature with man. And how elaborately he expresses it! We can almost hear the creaking of the literary machinery. He makes the beasts (excepting the fish—which would confuse the imagery) file before Adam for review. Now many have belittled Adam's intelligence just as many have exaggerated it, but he certainly recognized a brute when he saw one. And the real point the author wishes to make is that Adam at once saw that in all the odd procession there was no mate for him.

What is to be done? The Potter now becomes the Surgeon. Evidently the suitable material for woman's making is to be found in Adam himself. The Surgeon himself administers the narcotic and Adam sleeps. Why? Possibly, though this is a personal opinion, to bring out the element of waking surprise when the operation is over. You can almost see Adam jumping with delight as he cries, in words almost untranslatable:

Ah, this, *this time, is bone from my bones and flesh from my flesh!* This *shall be called WOMAN for from MAN* this *was taken!*

Woman may have become a chattel in the East but from the beginning, protests our author, it was not so. That God does not breathe into her "the breath of life" is of no significance at all: the breath is plainly in the living rib already. We shall speak further of this "rib" in the next chapter.

Such is the simple charter of Man's dignity. It might have been more sophisticated, it could not have been more profound. It enjoys, too, a pragmatic sanction. Man will forget it to his own undoing.

THE ANTHROPOLOGIST AND GENESIS

A FEW years ago, if one is to believe an old cutting from the
London *Times*, six live imported monkeys worried the
Board of British Customs not a little. The officials won, as
officials do, but the monkeys won too because they, that is
to say the monkeys, were proudly labelled not "quadruped" but "quadrumanous mammal". Each monkey, it
emerged, had twice as many hands as its owner who suffered
the added disadvantage of having to dip his into his pocket
and pay up. Now in this slightly irrelevant story there is
something that is to the point precisely because it is not
mentioned. I mean six passports. (Indeed, on a show of
hands, the officials might have demanded twelve.) The
officers at Folkestone, seemingly, did not even think of it.
And quite right too. Even the most extreme of our anthropologists would not have waived the Customs duty in favour
of a passport. You see, Man, whatever he may once have
been, is as yet the only animal in all creation who needs a
visa. This is the *present fact*. With facts it suits the laws of
Customs to deal. It suited Moses.

And because this viewpoint contented Moses it seems
important to protest against a certain tendency, which
might wrongly be thought a pious tendency, to invoke
Genesis in support of evolutionary theory. This is to fall
into the old error, christened "Concordism", which sought
to confer a B.Sc. upon Moses. It aimed at establishing
harmony between Genesis and the natural sciences not by
removing Genesis from the sphere of science but by

emphasizing the points of agreement.[1] We need scarcely say that those who valiantly attempted this reconciliation used the term "evolution" (as we shall use it) in the sense of "theistic evolution"; that is to say of evolutionary theory which takes account of a personal, transcendent Cause, which we call "God". Nothing less than this would satisfy Hebrew religious thought. The idea of a universe driving with evident purpose to a goal without a directive, transcendent Cause is unacceptable to a sound philosopher. It was quite unthinkable for the author of Genesis.

Now this error of Concordism was particularly unfortunate because it nourished a mistaken idea of Inspiration and of the intention of the inspired authors. We must say again as we have said before that Moses was not out to make pontifical pronouncements upon natural science; he was busy enough with his religious message. If any scrap of scientific information were truly necessary to this message, God, we claim, would have revealed it to him. Not otherwise. Therefore: if there is any evolutionary theory that has no necessary connection with religion, it will have to be judged on its own scientific merits. Inspiration, we repeat, guarantees every single *statement* of the sacred author—even his delicately hinted statements. Whatever its subject-matter—history, science, religion and the rest—such a statement has God's backing and God cannot be the guarantor of error in any sphere of knowledge. If we have an inspired scientific *statement*, that statement must be true. That is Catholic principle. But we must first make sure that we *have* a statement. Passing use of contemporary "scientific" notions to drive home a religious lesson can hardly be called a "statement" of these notions. That it is mere "passing use" should be clear from the purpose of the

---

[1] For an adroit and interesting approach to Genesis from the Concordist point of view cf. Robert, *Revue Biblique*, 1894, 387-401.

author which is a religious one and not scientific. Only if
the religious truth involved stands or falls by the accuracy
of the scientific information used will we expect a "statement" on the subject of science.

To return to Genesis: we see no connection between its
religious message and the exact way in which plants and
brutes came to be what they are. That God brought them
ultimately from nothing is enough. If, then, the inspired
author lets fall a phrase like: "Let the *earth bring forth
living creatures*", I shall not seize upon it as divine
testimony to the evolution of the beasts. I could only do so
if I were first to prove that the author, against all probability and against his usual custom, intends to make a
deliberate statement of this scientific titbit. He may be
using certain rough-and-ready evolutionary notions of
his time but this is far from categorically *affirming* them.
When the second Epistle of Peter (iii. 12) speaks of the
world's ending in terms of fire, he uses—but does not
teach—the speculations of the Graeco-Roman world.
It is therefore of little interest to the exegete that the
"cooling-down" theory of the nineteenth century has
now given place, in some scientific circles interested
in radio-activity, to a "warming-up" hypothesis. The
prudent exegete does not shout for joy at the news. For
once he sits back comfortably with benign detachment,
leaving the clever ones to do the work and marvelling at
Peter's new (and unneeded) champions.

By hauling Moses out of the deep blue sea of Science,
have we also delivered him from the devil of Anthropology? It would seem so, for anthropology is a science.
Alas, it is not so easy; for anthropology is the science of
Man. Cats, now, or dogs cannot fairly claim a place in
the Catechism nor a niche in Dogma—but Man? Ah,
this is where religion comes in; because what is religion
but Man kissing the chain that binds him to God? The

mettle of that chain cannot be a matter of indifference to a religious writer. It *may* be that he is interested in every link of it—even in the Missing Link. Not for its own scientific sake, of course, but for its religious implications. To speak more clearly: it *may* happen that the inspired author deliberately teaches, and therefore unerringly teaches, some truth related to man's origin which is not acceptable to a large majority of anthropologists. What are we to do if such a case should arise? We might first ask the anthropologist to re-examine his evidence and his reasoning. Having done this we shall go away quietly to make sure that we have got our own principles right and that we have applied them correctly. I say "go away" because we and they may be better apart for a while. The exegete has learned caution from the Galileo affair but he has the right to hope that it has not gone to the scientist's head. Old dogmas of the scientist have been quietly shelved before now. Neither party must be hasty. The truth is many-sided. Let me tell you a story. Once upon a time two armed and mounted knights, prying o'er the plain from opposite directions, halted *vis-à-vis*, a painted trophy between them. "Argent," said one. "Or," said the other. And they fought. And in the charge they crossed. "Or, perdi!" shouted the one. "Argent, i'faith," cried the other. For one side of the trophy was silver and the other gold. And they kissed and were friends.

One sometimes feels the need of protest when texts are being racked to extort an artificial confession. No author, not even an inspired author, should be forced to give more than he intends to give. We have two texts particularly in mind:

Let us make man to our own image and likeness: and let him have dominion over the fishes . . . and the fowls . . . and the beasts, and the whole earth.

This is from the first creation account of Genesis i. 1–
ii. 4a. In form it is as like the second account (Gen.
ii. 4b–24) as ruled graph-paper is like a painted canvas.
Compare it with the vivid second account:

And the Lord God fashioned man of dust from the soil,
And breathed into his face the breath of life
And man became a living person.

Both texts have their share of the picturesque and,
after all our discussions on "literary forms", it will
scarcely savour of paradox if we observe that the more
detailed text may well be the less helpful. Here especially
we shall have to be sensitive to the danger of taking our
sketch for a blueprint. But there is an observation,
connected with this last, that should be made; it is of
great moment and it bears directly on our present case.
It is this: *the author of each text is looking backwards.* In the
foreground of his present experience he sees Man *as he is,*
here and now. In the background, which is provided by
revelation, he sees God, Man's Creator. The distance,
if any, between foreground and background would be
foreshortened. God could have filled it in for the sacred
author by means of revelation, had he considered it of
any religious importance. He did not. This was possibly
because there was no distance to fill in, possibly because
this filling-in process was only a scientific operation that
could be performed in due time by honest men using
their God-given intellect. Remembering this possibility
of foreshortening let us consider the texts.

The author of the first has been struck by Man's position
in the scale of Being. This is hardly surprising since his
account of the whole Creation has shown us his passion
for order. From revelation he knows that one God is
Master of Man; from experience he knows that Man is

master of the beasts. Naturally enough he concludes
that Man is a little mirror of God; made, that is, to
God's "image and likeness". Had he put this as baldly
as I have done, everybody—I think—would have
recognized the foreshortening, the leap backwards from
Man as he is to God who made him so, without concern
for *how* God made him so. Yet our author has been
dragged into the Evolution affair. Why? Just because
he has used a pleasant literary device to enliven his
account. He had a statement to make about Man's
present status and about the Cause of this present
status. That God's deliberate act was the cause of this
status, the author is divinely assured. But the form he
chooses for expressing this truth is a graphic form. It is
the form of a sentence put into the mouth of God. The
effect is immediate and unavoidable. The great background, which is God, moves forward annihilating
distance. We feel suddenly that we and the author are
present at the whole business of Man's making. The
literary operation is dramatically sound but it may put us
in exegetical danger. Danger of thinking we have heard
the whole story—danger, therefore, of excluding the
possibility of human evolution on the grounds that it is
not mentioned.

The second text, too, works backwards from Man as he
is. And here again its circumstantial character might lure
us into forgetting the necessary foreshortening. But,
unlike the first, it sees Man's frail nature under the robes
of his dignity. The author is forced to it: the sad story of
the Fall is already in his mind. Man shall die and return
to dust (Gen. iii. 19); the author well knows it: he has
seen men breathing their last and their bones crumbling
to powder. He knows that dust and breath of life are
Man's equation. Yet the moulding of the dust and the
breathing of the breath are of God. That is the sub-

stance of the author's thought. Through what years and what strange forms this shaping dust felt the hands of the Eternal, he does not hint. Time and change are nothing to him before the two great realities: Man as he is and God as he has always been.

What, then? Do the texts say *nothing* of the "how" of Man's becoming? Not directly. It is true that the "Let us make man" of the first account stands in sharp contrast with the almost careless "Let the earth bring forth beasts". It is true that there is the same contrast in the second where God breathes the breath of life into man but not into the brutes (Gen. ii. 7, 19). But, we confess, we see little more in this than a literary effort to bring out what we would call the "specific difference" between Man and his fellow creatures. I say "little more" only because we are discussing the evolutionary theory but in the scale of real values it is already "very much"— so much, indeed, that the question of evolution becomes entirely secondary. The simple and sound philosophy of the inspired author points to what we should call the principle of intelligence in Man which establishes between him and the brutes a bridgeless gulf. It is highly probable, to say the least, that the idea of human evolution had never crossed the author's mind but his unsophisticated hints remain pertinent today. Before a theory of bodily evolution he might merely have rubbed his chin but he would have protested loudly against any attempt to present Man as nothing but an admirable development of the brute. His retort would have been, had he been born much later than he was: "The crowning perfection of this evolutionary process (if evolution there was) was the insertion, or more precisely the manifestation, of the intelligent soul, which cannot be regarded as the final stage of that process because it is, of its nature, impervious to the investigations of palaeontology and biology. It is

this association (of body with soul), an association lying
well outside the reach of scientific evolution, that produces
the new thing which we know as 'Man'. It answers,
therefore, to the theological doctrine of Man's Creation at
the hand of God." [1] And what fun his poor readers would
have had with language like that!

Now for some trouble:

*And the Lord God built the rib which He took from Adam into
a woman. . . . Wherefore a man shall . . . cleave to his wife:
and they shall be two in one flesh* (cf. Gen. ii. 22–24).

Of course, our general principle still holds good: it is still
true that the author's purpose is to insist upon the divine
establishment of things *as they are*—the status of women,
this time. He is still not primarily interested in the mode
of their becoming. He is convinced of the essential equality
of the sexes, of the subordinate function of woman, of the
stability of the marriage-bond. The author certainly
wishes to say that these things are of God. But does he
wish to say more? Does he intend more than a fanciful
parable of all these things? Does he really mean that the
physical Eve was formed from a part of Adam's organism?
If so, how do I prove it? What right have I to say that
our author, hitherto disdainful of natural science, has
suddenly changed his policy?

A tender question indeed and one that beseeches
exegetical *finesse*. Perhaps the time is not ripe for an
answer. If we suggest one we do so very, very tentatively
and reserving the right to revise it. Let us put the argument this way: our passage gives us the impression that
the author is going out of his way (this time!) to *teach* us
something in the line of anthropology—the physical

[1] cf. Vincent, O.P., in *Revue Biblique*, 1950, 134.

origin of the first woman. How do we get this impression? From the highly circumstantial nature of the story? No: even a parable—I might have said "especially a parable"—may be elaborately contrived. How then? From the author's own hint. *"For this reason"*, says he (i.e. because woman was taken from man), "they shall be two in one flesh." His conclusion is within the order of morality and therefore well within a religious author's scope. But, and here is the point, *he appears also to depend for this conclusion upon a physiological fact*. We do not say that it would have been impossible for him to formulate his conclusion in this way had the account of Eve's formation been merely a parable, as Cajetan suggested in the sixteenth century, or just Adam's subjective vision, as Hummelauer held in the nineteenth. We say only that it would be strange. If, then, we are to take the more natural explanation of the text it would seem that the author intends to make a statement upon a scientific fact. The statement is not made for its own sake, of course, but because it is intimately connected with a moral issue. Hence when the Biblical Commission sustains the "literal historical" truth of this incident it is simply safeguarding the apparent intention of the sacred author.

Now very few anthropologists would be prepared to concede the evolution of only one of the sexes and the "special creation" of the other. This being so, it is not surprising if our passage has given many a headache to certain Catholics, a not inconsiderable number, who have some sympathy for the evolutionary hypothesis. Some gloss over this particular difficulty, others admit that explanations so far attempted are all but grotesque. Another assigns to Adam an active part in the production of Eve, rather against the tone of the Genesis account, and suggests a process "analogous to the phenomenon of a-sexual generation so frequent in the animal kingdom".[1] It should, however, be remarked that this phenomenon is found only in the lower orders of the animal kingdom.[2]

A brief word about the "rib". In the Biblical Commission's list of subjects whose "literal historical truth" may not be called in question we find "the formation of the first woman from the first man" but no mention whatever of the "rib". This may or may not be one of the "metaphorical elements" to which a later paragraph of the decree refers. But if the incident as a whole is to be given an historical interpretation, as we have shown to be likely on purely rational grounds, then there would seem to be little point, or even warrant, in taking this single element metaphorically. After all, why not a rib? A divine surgeon would supply Adam's lack and "rib" is probably the correct translation of the Hebrew word which is used also of the side of the Ark of Covenant, for the planks of the Tabernacle, etc.

It is not time for a final verdict. The case is still *sub judice* and many witnesses, buried in the ground or deep in the sacred text, have not yet been called. We should end with a firm little parenthesis: (*Proceeding*). But may we sum up the case as it stands? To be frank our first instinct is to mistrust efforts to *subpoena* Genesis in the interests of either litigating party. It may be said, in the present state of exegesis and of anthropology which are both developing sciences, that "the hypothesis of full creation squares better with the story of Genesis taken as a whole".[3] But then, of course, this is to be expected of an author who has no other hypothesis in mind. Moreover, the picturesque character of the Genesis

---

[1] Messenger, *Evolution and Theology*, 1931, 269-273.
[2] cf. Lagrange, *Revue Biblique*, 1932, 462.
[3] Lagrange in the article just quoted.

narrative makes it rash to urge that the inspired text is clearly opposed to "baptized evolution", as Catholic evolutionary theory has been dubbed. It is clear, I hope, that we have not made it our business to discuss the precisely theological aspect of the question. That must be left to the trained theologian. We have tried to throw some light only into one corner of the dark problem— the corner filled by the first chapters of Genesis. We have suggested that they stand outside the controversy—with the possible exception of the passage dealing with Eve's formation. Of this passage a recent Catholic commentary remarks that "it appears to exclude the hypothesis of evolution in any form" though the same writer had declared some years before that the "baptized evolution" hypothesis was matter "not for exegesis but for anthropology".[1] We have just heard Lagrange's opinion; from another school of Catholic exegesis comes a more severe sentence: "The story of Genesis is far from friendly (*minime favet*) to even the most moderate form of evolutionary theory."[2] But the exegetes are far from unanimous and the new Supplement to the *Dictionnaire de la Bible*, for instance, consigns the question to the scientists.[3]

As for the Catholic theologians it is plain that they have hitherto not welcomed the theory even in its most moderate form. This opposition is partly explained, but only partly, by the unfortunate fact that the hypothesis of human evolution has so often been firmly—we might add arbitrarily"—harnessed to an atheistic or a pantheistic chariot.[4]

The recent Letter of the Commission to Cardinal

[1] P. F. Ceuppens, O.P., *Genèse I-III*, 1946, p. 137; cf. the same author's *Historia Primaeva*, 1934, p. 133.
[2] A. Bea, S.J., *De Pentateucho*, 1933, p. 154f.
[3] Pirot, *Dictionnaire de la Bible, Supplément*, 1928, i, 94.
[4] Among the theologians, Pesch, S.J., *Compendium Theologiae Dogmaticae*, '13, ii, 161; Van Noort, *De Deo Creatore*, 1920, pp. 113-132; Boyer, S.J., *De Deo Creante et Elevante*, 1929, pp. 142-162, are unfavourable.

Suhard emphasizes the "popular" character of the sacred account of human origins and asks for a further examination of the religious problems involved. It also recalls the words of the Holy Father in which the Catholic exegete is urged to solutions which, while fully respecting the Church's doctrine, will take adequate account of the *proved* conclusions of the natural sciences. It is an invitation no true Catholic will refuse.[1]

[1] The Letter is dated Jan. 16, 1948; cf. *Acta Apostolicae Sedis*, series II, XV, 45-48.

XI

GENESIS AGAIN: SERPENTS AND THINGS

FOR OVER fifty years people have been staring at a Babylonian cylinder-seal in the British Museum. Let me introduce it to you. Centre: a stiff and schematic tree; right: human figure on camp-stool and wearing horns; left: human figure on camp-stool and wearing beret (well, very like); wavy line rising upwards behind left-hand figure; both figures, if you discount the beret, decently dressed. "Oho!" say the impetuous, "the Babylonian story of the Fall." "Mmmm," says the scholar, who has been caught before, "why clothes? Why horns—a sign of divinity; is it a man after all? Why beret—is it a woman? Why wavy line—is it a serpent?" And there the affair rests. But you see the need for caution where angels tread delicately. Surface-likenesses are tempting but deceitful things. I recall a row of baby faces in some Sunday paper; readers were asked to identify the famous adults who had owned them. Many of us recognized the future Archbishop of Canterbury in the infant features of Adolf Hitler.

This by way of warning only. You will not conclude, I hope, that the whole *mise en scène* of the biblical story of the Fall stands splendidly isolated in the literature of the ancient East. Why should the sacred writers disdain the common fund of oriental imagery? In fact they do not disdain it. Enchanted gardens, trees of lapis lazuli, guardian cherubim, serpents—all these the archaeologist has found already; and there is more to come. What, then? Myth in the Bible? No, but the secondary apparatus of myth. Let me explain.

A few years ago (about four thousand) a story was going round Babylonia—a story of an ancient king of Erech which lies some seventy miles north and east of Abraham's home-town of Ur. He was an ancient king even when the story knew him, because he was of the second dynasty of Erech after the Deluge. Abraham must have heard this long yarn in his native place. Moreover, the wandering minstrels of the day, whose existence is considered highly probable, must have chanted it far from home in the camps and courts of Canaan. Now of this hero they sang many songs and one concerns us. Scared nigh to death, goes the chant, our Gilgamish seeks the plant of immortality. Tying stones to his feet and removing the bottom of the boat which, in its friendly fashion, still floats, he plucks the herb from the sea's bed. But on his triumphant way home being minded to bathe in a cold pool he leaves his plant on the bank. A serpent smells it and swallows it. And Gilgamish sits down and cries.

Now that is a good story though sad. It reminds us of another we have heard in which man is robbed of immortality by a serpent—and robbed of other things too. But side by side with Genesis it is a blown egg. For the sake of argument let us forgive its more highly tinted shell; what nourishment does it afford us? None, though much amusement. Cleanliness, they say, is neighbour to godliness, so it was through no fault of poor Gilgamish that he lost his hardly-won herb. So far I have met no one for whom the great Epic is canonical scripture, but when I do I shall ask him what lesson he has picked up from the conduct of Gilgamish. And he will answer, this simple soul, that he now takes no risk with cold water and (probably) that he doesn't walk under ladders either. You see, the story is of magic, not of morality. It will teach you superstition and no more. But Genesis? Ah, the hands may be the hands of Gilgamish but the voice is the authentic voice of Israel. We say "Poor Gilgamish!" but who says "Poor Adam"? It was Adam's deliberate fault, not his unearned misfortune. If we miss this most solid fact we may as well close our Bible. The climate of the Genesis story is entirely moral. When Adam names the beasts he displays intelligence; when God gives the precept he supposes the use of reason; when the serpent suggests the sin he appeals to argument; when God pronounces sentence he imputes responsibility. Here is morality and not magic. Here is profound ethical monotheism—a stern and stiff and lonely thing amid the mad frolic of the surrounding polytheistic myths. If Genesis has borrowed the old tune it has written brand-new words.

The old tune? Dangerous, surely! Perilous flirting with pagan forms! Perilous indeed—unless a monotheism perfectly sure of itself found those forms harmless at last. With a like confidence we recite in our breviary:

From the high top of Olympus the Father's Son descends.

St. Paul would have hated his Greek converts to hear that; but nowadays we know how to borrow the mountain of the gods without adopting the mythology of the Greeks. Just as confidently Isaias dips his hand into the Phoenician bag and pulls out gems to stud his plaque of Babylon's fall:

> How thou art fallen from heaven,
> Daystar, son of Dawn!
> Thou who hast said in thy heart:
> "I shall take my seat upon the Mount of the Council
> Away in the distant North! . . .
> I shall be like to the Most High". (Isa. xiv. 13, 14.)

E

Are we to suspect this satirical Isaias (Isaias!) of poly-theism? Stout monotheist as he is he plays with "Day-star", father of the goddesses, and with "Dawn", son of the high god El. It suits the irony of hell's song of wel-come to fallen Babylon.[1] And you will notice that Isaias, like Ezechiel (Ezech. i. 4; xxviii. 14), is not timid of referring to the mountain of the gods' council which, again in Phoenician myth, lies in the far north. In cases like this the myth recedes and leaves its phrases behind. Thus the Psalmist (Ps. xlvii. 3) does not blush to borrow this same mythical hill and to dub the holy city of Sion, whose latitude he knew well enough, "Distant North". The new Knox version is shrewd enough when it freely renders: "True pole of earth", but "Heaven on earth" or "World's Olympus" would have done as well.

Evidently the day dawns when the waste paper of myth may be safely re-pulped; when the pernicious stuff has been sterilized and has lost its poison. I think we Christians speak, for example, of Thor's Day without a qualm. We use these things, alien as they are, for our convenience. We have made some very fine chasubles from wedding dresses.

You see whither we are driving? "Stop!" cries Wary, "this is much too glib. When the serpent creeps into Gilgamish you howl: 'Nonsense!' When he crawls into Genesis you murmur: 'Symbol!'. What special pleading is this?" "You wrong me, sir [I reply]; you imply that I deny symbol to Gilgamish. I do not. I know all too little of the mentality of these old singers or of the origin of their songs." But the real question is whether the thing symbolized is more important than the symbol. Now let us generously concede that the serpent of the Gilgamish

---

[1] " Daystar " is " Lucifer " in the Vulgate. It is from this passage, applied by many of the Fathers to the fall of Satan, that the devil gets one of his names which (were it not ironical) is all too complimentary.

Epic *is* a symbol. What does it symbolize? Slippery chance—*any* slippery chance. Now a real, physical serpent would be himself a slippery chance, no less. I therefore conclude that the Epic had nothing *more important* in mind than a physical serpent. With Genesis the case is vastly different. There, as we have seen, the serpent fills the rôle of a moral force, not of an unhappy accident. Remove the serpent-mask and there is the face of the Force more terrible than the mask. Remove the serpent from Gilgamish and nothing remains but an alternative accident.

In short, the profundity beneath the simplicity of the Genesis narrative demands that we credit its author with a sense of proportion. It invites us, commands us, to believe that an author who soared so high above his contemporaries—indeed he thought on another plane—surpassed them no less in estimating the true value of his thought-forms than he did in rejecting the old nonsense those forms had once clothed. Less pedantically: he knew his symbols to be symbols and nothing more.

We must insist that this conclusion is probable on purely rational grounds. We are not grinding a theological axe. In fact, one would like to add, it is doubtful if the doctrine of Inspiration, rightly understood, would *demand* such a conclusion. One of the consequences of Inspiration is guaranteed truth. But truth, or error, dwells only in formal judgment. Now formal judgment is concerned not with the "proper" (as opposed to the "transferred") literal sense of metaphors, symbols, etc., but with the objective realities underlying them. It *may be*, therefore, that the inspired author is not always conscious that he is using mere symbol, etc. However, the question is delicate and the suggestion we have made remains a suggestion. It goes without saying that it is submitted to the Church's judgment.

But why did the sacred author—or perhaps Satan himself—choose a snake for his tool of expression? It is perhaps sufficient to answer that we all hate snakes anyway. It is already half an answer to explain that the writer, like a good pedagogue, was using an image familiar—perhaps from Gilgamish—to his readers. But there is a little more in it than that. You must know that, in the ancient East, the serpent was a *beneficent* djinn. He was the wise one—"most astute of all the animals *that God had made*" (but note that!), says Genesis. He was said to hold the key of all magical knowledge and the secret of life. An upright gentleman too—I mean in the physical sense. In ancient pictures if he is not standing on his own feet he is curled round a tree or poised on his tail. He was thought very highly of in Canaan and wormed his way even into Israelitic hearts so that king Ezechias, in the eighth century, was compelled to smash the abused bronze serpent of Moses. Now suppose an *author* wished to smash the serpent? What better way to scotch an adored snake than by making him a villain of his piece? By making him the cause of all man's ills and the lying claimant to knowledge? A defeated villain, too—pulled down from his vaunted uprightness by the simple word of Yahweh: "Down on thy belly!" Not a bad way of putting a pestiferous god where he belonged!

Since curiosity about this animal is so lively we may permit ourselves a short digression. We have used terms which suppose that it is the author who gives the Tempter the form of a serpent. Nevertheless we should notice that what has been said demonstrates the aptness of the form chosen whether it be chosen only by the author or actually assumed by the Tempter himself. Either the author or Satan deems it suitable. Which? In this point a decree of the Biblical Commission is pertinent (published in 1909; cf. Denzinger-Bannwart, 2123). Before we examine it, it would be well to point out that these decrees are not hastily worded. From the very nature of the case and from experience their learned authors are fully aware that the words will go under a microscope and they pick their words accordingly. Their care is motived by the gravity of the subject which is nothing less than the dignity and understanding of God's word and by the fact that their decrees, though not irrevocable, command the assent of all Catholic exegetes. Catholic scholars may submit arguments for revision of such decrees but unless and until that revision is made the decrees remain in full force. From all this it is clear that commonsense and loyalty alike bid us scrutinize the terms with the utmost diligence. Such diligence applied to casual statements would be mere word-chopping; in the law-court it is the sifting of evidence; here it is a religious duty.

The purpose of the decree is to safeguard "the facts which have to do with ['attingunt'] the foundations of the Christian religion". Amongst these facts is numbered: "the transgression at the instigation of the devil under the guise of a [the?] serpent" ("diabolo sub specie serpentis suasore"). Now in view of the declared purpose of the decree it is plain that the emphasis is thrown on "devil", not on "serpent", because the "guise of serpent" would scarcely seem to "touch upon the foundations of the Christian religion". It is evident, on the other hand, why the Commission should insist that the Tempter was in fact the power of evil ("devil"). Such insistence guards the moral value of the story against the superficial theory that the author was out to explain merely natural phenomena as, for instance, the horizontal posture of serpents and man's instinctive horror of them. The decree declares that though the author says "serpent" he means much more—what appears as serpent is in fact devil. We may therefore, it seems, interpret the decree: "at the instigation of the devil

presented to us in the narrative under the guise of serpent"
—i.e. under the *literary* form (symbol) of serpent.

At this stage comes the fair question: "Why this itch
for symbolism? You have proved that we *may* symbolize,
but *must* we? Why not accept the simple story with simple
faith? Are you just trying to make things easier for the
sophisticated?" The answer is a thousand times "No".
Such procedure would be exegetical dishonesty, and as for
simple Faith (with a capital "F")—if the scholar has it not,
then heaven help the scholar. It does indeed seem that one
half of the so-called difficulties against Faith are difficulties
only against Imagination. By removing the "fruit" or the
"serpent", say, from Genesis, I do in fact remove the strain
on the imagination. But does it make Faith any easier?
In any case, the removal of the strain must be accidental
for the honest interpreter, though, on God's part, it may be
providential. Please absolve me from the charge of
"making things easier". For the man who quaintly
discovered that the Real Presence defied chemical analysis
it would have "made things easier" had he studied
the Thomistic doctrine of the Holy Eucharist. We
shall not, however, accuse St. Thomas of having
this purpose in mind. The fact is that truth is sometimes "easier" than falsehood. Come, now; back to our
point.

We have mentioned the "fruit". It is possible that the
fruit was a real one and the whole incident a mere test-case.
There are schools from which a boy has been expelled for
putting a herb into his mouth and setting a flame to it. Why
not something of the kind as a test for primitive human-
ity? It may be so. Yet it should be noticed that the cases
are not truly parallel. In certain cases a superior is out to
test a boy's obedience to *human* authority and when this
is his purpose he is forced to select some action which is
not already covered by the law of God. The selection is

perforce what we should call "arbitrary". Adam's situation was vastly different. God alone was his "superior". What need for an "arbitrary" command? Commands enough were already implicit in Adam's condition as a creature—gratitude and reverence towards his Creator, for instance. We expect, therefore, that the sin would be some flagrant violation of Adam's creature-status. Such expectation may smack of theology but we have seen, I hope, that our author is no mean theologian himself. He seeks the first cause of all man's sinwardness and sinfulness. When he finds it, I venture to think, he will find the most capital of capital sins because even setting revelation aside he is not naïve. In our next essay we shall try to discover what that sin was.

XII

MAN'S SIN

Paracelsus : I am he that aspired to KNOW; and thou?
Aprile : I would LOVE infinitely and be loved.
Paracelsus : Poor slave! I am thy king indeed.

(Browning. *Paracelsus*.)

Happy is he that wisdom gains and skill;
Yet he is no match for one who fears the Lord.

(Ecclesiasticus xxv. 13. Knox Version.)

TRUE LOVE has a quality that makes it a very sane thing
and safe. It thrusts outward. It is first the forgetfulness,
then the contempt, then the repudiation of the Self. Needless to say, this order must be reversed if you seek spiritual
practice and not theoretical crescendo. The whole
process is known by the terrifying term : "self-denial"—
an expression worn and worn to a polish, alas, from
its primitive roughness. But as for knowledge, now, the
case is different—not of necessity but in common human
experience. Heaven forbid that we should wage war on
knowledge but it is true to say that learning is not as safe as
loving. Where love flies forth like an arrow knowledge
comes back like a boomerang : it may go humbly to school
but it comes home proudly hugging its books. It is a conscious perfecting of the self, not a "denial" of the self. It
does indeed threaten humility. It is easy to come to think
that knowledge:

> Rather consists in opening out a way
> Whence the imprisoned splendour may escape,
> Than in effecting entry for the light.

The inspired writers themselves, in certain moods, seem to have their suspicions of human science. They appear to wonder, as we sometimes wonder, if human wisdom can keep pace with human wit. Science rushes the doctor to the bedside but does it leave a corpse on the roadside? And the Babel tower was a massive feat of engineering but God is shown frowning at the builders. Nor is it perhaps without significance that Genesis ascribes the invention of the technical arts to the sons of the accursed Cain—which name is possibly equivalent to the English "Smith". Not that the science of nature is condemned; on the contrary: the encyclopaedic knowledge of Solomon is commended in the Book of Wisdom (vii. 17ff). But the sacred authors feel that the tool is unsafe in the hands of those not possessed of the fountain head of true wisdom which is the fear of the Lord. We might be forgiven for observing, in passing, that the nineteenth century might have smiled at this but not the twentieth—certainly not the twentieth. This mistrust of sheerly human progress is well symbolized by Miss Sayers in an admirable Mystery-play: Adam is delighted with his first axe but, in the hand of Cain, it fells not trees but his son.

"Knowledge is Power", says an advertisement. So it is. Let me know a dog's name and I shall control him. Hebrew and many another psychology followed the same lines. Thus the mysterious thing that wrestles with Jacob withholds its name in order to escape Jacob's power. In the same way Adam's naming of the beasts demonstrates his control of them. Now it is important to bear in mind this very practical view of knowledge when we are faced with the phrase: *Knowledge of Good and Evil*, the phrase that lies at the heart of the story of the Fall. Whatever this Knowledge is it will not be a purely speculative thing—it will be a reaching after power of some sort. In the mind of the Hebrew author Adam did not seek merely the satisfaction of his abstract intellect. For this reason alone one is inclined to reject the theory that Adam sought the omniscience which was God's exclusive property. But the opinion becomes positively untenable if we remember, as we have already said so often, that the writer sets himself to explain the state of man *as he is*—and he knows well enough that man is not omniscient.

G. B. Shaw, like many another popular writer, favours a more picturesque view in his *Back to Methuselah*. This is not surprising. It is what could be described as "good theatre" or, as a scholar dubbed it less kindly some fifty years ago, "l'exégèse de l'Opéra Comique". According to this opinion the "knowledge of good and evil" is what is rather stupidly called the knowledge of "the facts of life"—of the nature and purpose of marriage. This is a typical example of what we might call "retroactive" exegesis. It reads into an ancient author the pseudo-prudery of a later age. It was Galsworthy and not Genesis who used the smart and superficial phrase: "a rather naughty sacrament". The sacred writer who has just registered the divine blessing and command: "Increase and multiply", the Hebrew who knows that "the fruitful womb is the reward that comes from Him" is a man of robust mind.[1] The modern age may examine its conscience but *he* had no need to be ashamed of matrimony.

But there is an allied, more sophisticated and more useful school of thought. Recalling, quite rightly, that the word "Adam" means "man" it suggests that the whole story of the Fall was never meant to be a history but rather an allegory of every man's experience from cradle to grave. In this sense, Adam and Eve first appear as children. The paradise-happiness of childhood sees no prospect of death. It is innocent and without self-consciousness. Then comes the fatal thirst for knowledge

[1] Gen. i. 28; Ps. cxxvi, Knox Version.

"Why? Why??" With knowledge comes disillusion-ment and disappointment. Then adolescence with its consequences. Work follows next—thorns and thistles in place of toys. "And then from hour to hour we rot and rot" and death becomes a real and personal prospect. All very dismal. All very true, too, and doubtless it passed through the author's mind. Certainly such thoughts have a lesson for us: "Each man", says a Jewish author a century before Christ, "is an Adam for himself".

Yet all this, though instructive, is a side-issue. It is not to be confused with the primary purpose of the author which, whatever some may think of the truth of the story, is to give a factual—if vivid—*explanation* of our human state, not a mere *tableau* of it. It is clear that the author intends to describe not a development which takes place in all of us willy-nilly but a deliberate fault which induced its own punishment. We shall see in a moment that Adam does really achieve the "knowledge of good and evil"; when he does so it is certainly not the gift of conscience that he wins because this would be in no sense a fault whereas the whole narrative implies a fault. Nor is it an awareness of moral good and moral evil towards which he inevitably evolves: no Hebrew author in his senses would imply that God withheld this awareness from man ("Of the tree of knowledge of good and evil thou shalt not eat!").

The process of showing what a thing is not never fails to annoy. The apprentice-gunner is always irritated at the waste of his first two shells. Yet it is necessary range-finding and we have not been wasting our time. At this stage we know at least that the account of the Fall is meant to be the history of a fact. We know also that the sinister desire for "knowledge" was neither ambition of omniscience nor curiosity anent "the facts of life". What remains? Recall the witnesses!

First: "Thou shalt not eat!" This is God's express

command. On this unshakable evidence we have firmly dismissed the charge against Marriage and Conscience.

Second: "Ye shall be as gods knowing good and evil". This time it is the Serpent speaking from the witness-box. He has a bad record but, the jury will remember, criminals may turn king's evidence. It may be true that Adam and his wife will, in their very act of consent, "be as gods". (We should here remark that the word "angels" would here better express the Hebrew *'elohim*.[1] Critics agree that the author is no polytheist. The plural "us" in the next quotation is to be similarly explained: God associates his court with his administration.)

Third: "Behold Adam is become like one of us, knowing good and evil". This is God's evidence again—confirming the Serpent's. In "knowing good and evil" man really did become "like God"

This conclusion is at first sight so remarkable that many have refused, and not a few still refuse, the evidence on which it is based. The Serpent lies—so runs the argument —and God is ironical. If this is true it is clear that our witnesses numbered "two" and "three" are valueless or rather positively antagonistic to our conclusion. But we would quarrel mildly at least with the second of these two statements: that God's words are ironical. After all, irony has to be proved. It is betrayed normally by stress of tone or curl of lip. Now a disembodied text has neither tone nor lip. The irony of a text, therefore, can appear only from its intrinsic absurdity if taken seriously and not ironically. It follows that if the words :- "Adam is become like one of us" can be shown to contain no intrinsic absurdity then the case for irony stands unproved.

Before we attempt to demonstrate that these words are capable of a straightforward and serious interpretation we should not leave without mention a new translation

[1] cf. Skinner, *Genesis*, p. 75; cf. also *Verbum Domini*, 1949, pp. 278-285.

recently proposed by Canon Coppens of Louvain: "Behold Adam, *like each one who will be born of him*, will undergo the experience of ('know') good and evil". The italicized words replace our "like one of us" and it is plain that this new version would change the whole situation since that phrase is crucial in our argument. It is fair and prudent to record this opinion even at the risk of confusion but it suffers the grave difficulty, among others, of translating the Hebrew Perfect tense: "*has* become . . . knowing" as a Future: "*will* know ('undergo') . . .".[1]

Well, then, we submit the following odd verdict: that man in wishing to be like God ran counter to God's will and, moreover, that man succeeded in his design. I say the verdict is odd for two reasons. First, because God deliberately made man to his own likeness and because this likeness was to be man's high destiny: "We shall be like him because we shall see him as he is".[2] In the second place it is strange that man should succeed in usurping the jealously-guarded prerogative of God. We hope that both of these riddles will be resolved by the explanation which is now about to be proposed.

Adam's ambition was for knowledge—for practical knowledge, a knowledge that enables action like the knowledge of how to use a handsaw. Now this action was action in the moral order and not in the merely physical, as the moral climate of the story shows. So far, so good. Do we not ourselves laudably seek to know the ultimate principles which lie behind and stimulate moral conduct? Is this not the whole business of the science of Ethics? Yes, but with this essential difference that in Ethics we seek the wisdom of God as manifested in his will regarding man's moral conduct. Adam, on the other hand, was fully aware,

---

[1] cf. the thorough review of Canon Coppens' book in *Revue Biblique*, 1949, 300-308, by R. de Vaux OP.
[2] I John iii. 2.

in this instance, that God's will was contrary to his ambition ("Thou shalt not eat!"). He was certainly not studying Ethics, therefore. That he was defying God's express prohibition shows that he was arrogating the privilege of deciding *for himself* what was morally good and what was morally evil and of acting according to that decision.[1] The decision, in these circumstances, is inevitably perverse because it is made against the only competent arbiter— God. Such defiant decision holds the essence of sin:

Woe to them that call evil "Good" and good "Evil". (Isa. v. 20.)

The peculiar malice of Adam's fault should be seen against a wider biblical background. Thus, for example, the great king Solomon prays for the knowledge of "good and evil":

Give to thy servant an understanding heart to judge thy people and discern between good and evil. (3 Kings iii. 9.)

On this occasion God makes no objection—indeed he is pleased. That he hears the prayer is straightway proved by the famous Solomon-and-Baby incident that immediatcly follows. What is it that the king has asked for? The gift of arbitration between what was good and what was evil. It was a truly royal quality of administration at a time when the king was both legislator and judge. According to the cunning woman of Thekua it was David's gift too:

As an angel of the Lord is my lord the king judging both good and evil. (From the Hebrew of 2 Sam. xiv. 17; cf. Douay Version 2 Kings xiv. 17.)

[1] This view is excellently presented and defended by Fr. de Vaux in the article just quoted. We have used some of his texts but his argument is too detailed to develop here.

We have here a significant echo of: "Ye shall be as gods (angels) knowing good and evil". But why is there no word of blame for Solomon or for David? What difference is there between Solomon and Adam? This: that Adam set himself up as arbiter of good and evil but Solomon asked humbly to be allowed to share the arbitration which he knew to belong to God alone. We have said that the distinction between good and evil is rooted in infinite wisdom. It may be communicated to man, as it was to Solomon; it must not be arrogated, as it was by Adam. When it is so communicated we know it as right conscience; when it is so usurped we know it as blasphemous arrogance. When God crowns, the diadem sits sweetly; it presents the authority of God and confers upon man the likeness to God in which man was created and to which he must ever further aspire. When man steals the crown it rests upon his brow as a heavy mockery and preludes death; the "likeness to God" is a caricature and the usurpation a great loss. Aquinas, therefore, puts the ultimate malice of the first sin in Pride:

The principal element in man's sin was in seeking to be like God precisely *by deciding for himself which actions were good and which bad.* (*Summa* II-II, 163, 2.)

Such appears to be the symbolism of the "fruit of knowledge". Too many have fastened on the "fruit" and forgotten the "knowledge of good and evil" which is, after all, the ruling phrase and which lives in the biblical tradition. This knowledge was meant for man indeed but it could only come from God. It was only God-given wisdom which "brought him out of his sin" in the end (Wisd. x. 2). With this great gift in mind the author of Ecclesiasticus who sings man's praises can now ignore and overleap man's first miserable attempt at independent "knowledge":

He made him to His image . . .
Gave him dominion of beast and bird . . .
Filled him with wisdom and understanding,
Made him to know good and evil. (Ecclus. xvii. 4ff.)

Pentecost was the undoing of Babel. When man sought unity and a rallying-point on his own initiative God did not approve. In the great affairs of man the initiative must lie with God: "Unless the Lord build the house . . .". The strange incident of Babel means this at least. But when the initiative does rest with God, chaos turns to order and internationalism becomes truly possible. When God proposed His world-society men exclaimed: "We have heard them speak in our own tongues!" (Acts ii. 11.) Man needs knowledge but a knowledge which is "according to God" if he is to build at all. Heaven knows we have seen this miserably proved in the councils of the nations. Use any jargon you like—call it a "common ethic"—but it is the God-given knowledge of good and evil. But if it is not God-given then it is not common and around the conference-table sit so many Adams determining each for himself what is good and what is evil. And they walk out one by one.

XIII

DIVERTIMENTO: BIBLICAL NUMBERS

The man looked at me as if he thought me a very wicked fellow; and, I dare say, has by this time discovered that if you write my name in Tamul, leaving out T in Thomas, B in Babington and M in Macaulay, it will give the number of this unfortunate beast.

(From the Letters of Lord Macaulay.)

ASSUREDLY the cabbalism of numbers is a dangerous sport. But the human mind insists; it will impose its patterns upon plainness; the pulse and lungs force chaos into rhythm. Where every pulse beats and every mind considers within its lonely dominion, what rich diversity! So with Macaulay and the English divine of Mysore. The Beast of the Apocalypse, said the divine, plainly means Buonaparte: "If you write Napoleon Buonaparte in Arabic, leaving out only two letters, it will give 666" (the number with which John branded the Beast). Macaulay was not impressed. "Sir", said he, "the House of Commons is the Beast. There are 658 members of the House; and these with their chief officers—the three clerks, the Sergeant and his deputy, the Chaplain, the doorkeeper and the librarian—make 666". And that, one would think, settles it. And yet it doesn't, you know.

Not that we intend to go chasing Jack-o'-lanterns: we know very well, and the principle is not alien to biblical interpretation, that some figures are not meant to be taken too literally. "A million times I go to sleep with you on my brain", writes a modern lyricist; but I have no quarrel with him, if little sympathy. I do not tax him with error or with deceit when it is solemnly pointed out that his statement implies that the crooner is at least two thousand three hundred and seventy-nine years of age. No, let us do the songwriter justice: there are certain numerical expressions which defy scrutiny. And the more "round" a number is the more it does defy it. "But beware! Our round may be another's square." In this the roundness of our zero plays its part—so do our fingers and toes. But what of those who prefer to quarter the round moon and so to think in terms of the seven days of the week?

And the children of Israel came into Elim where there were twelve fountains of water and seventy palm trees. (Exod. xv. 27.)

Exactly seventy? Or rather an approximation to express the fertility of the desert-station? Or did the child revived by Elias really sneeze seven times? Or did the author of Genesis know that Jacob bowed precisely seven times to Esau? (Gen. xxxiii. 3).

A venerable number this; highly thought of by all the ancients. It seemed so often to peep through creation. Seven planets, seven stars of the Great Bear, seven Pleiades, seven notes of the musical scale, seven sensory terminals in the human head—eyes, ears, nostrils, mouth. Small wonder if the Greek and Latin words for "seven" have their root common with the Greek word for "veneration" (*hepta, septem, sebasmos*) or if the Hebrew word "to take a solemn oath" has its radicals in common with the term for "seven". This odd number is always finding its way into Hebrew literature. It seems to fascinate St. Matthew who gives us seven parables in one chapter, seven "woes" in another, seven devils, seven loaves, seven baskets, seven petitions of the "Our Father" and—probably—seven beatitudes. For him this number has the roundness of

perfection and to forgive "seventy times seven times" is to
forgive abundantly and without end.

Knowing this we shall not be misled, for instance, by his
three series of "fourteen" generations in our Lord's
family-tree. He is quite aware that, among other things,
he has banished three kings of Juda from his second series.
He is aware because the source which he manifestly uses
(1 Par. iii. 15–16) certainly contains them. But Matthew
wanted a multiple of his beloved seven. Moreover, and it
seems more than happy accident, the number fourteen is
the numerical sum of the Hebrew consonants of David's
name (D W D : D being the fourth letter of the alphabet
and W the sixth). There are indications, too, that a three-
fold fourteen had messianic significance in Rabbinic
thought. It is a reasonable conclusion that Matthew is
presenting his Messias, son of David, as the David *par
excellence*. Confirmation comes from the Apocalypse where
the whole Christian, messianic, era appears as a period of
thrice fourteen months (Apoc. xi. 2; xiii. 5). It is true
also that the holy name of Jesus occurs exactly fourteen
times in this same book but it is possible that in this we
have simple though strange chance.

Before we return to our Beast, who was registered as
666, I must show you that from the number seven which
we have just been discussing to the number 666 is not such
a far cry.

The horseleech has three daughters [who cry]: *"Give; give!"
and four who never say: "Enough!"*. (Prov. xxx. 15, emended.)

The inspired author wishes to say that the bloodsucker,
image of greedy death, has an infinity of thirsty mouths.
The impression of multitude is achieved by repeating the
first round number with a unit added. Though it is rather
by the way we might here recall a similar device of the
Psalmist:

God has spoken one thing; these two have I heard: To God is the
power, and the favour thine, O Lord. (Ps. lxi. 12.)

The effect here is to throw weight on to the second number;
as we might say a thing could not be done "in a month,
aye in a year, of Sundays". The attention of the reader
of the psalm is thus drawn to the sharp distinction between
"power" and "favour"—the second half of the second
line of the quotation is not to be taken, therefore, as a
mere pious repetition of the first half.

We now come back to the similar but not identical trick
of the sentence from Proverbs. In that sentence addition of
a unit implied abundance; what will subtraction signify?
Something imperfect—even sinister. (Subtract one from
the first multiple of seven and you have our "unlucky"
13.) How miserly and miserable are subtraction and
division! How joyous and open-handed their opposites!
Daniel cuts seven in half for misery:

And they [God's chosen people] *shall be delivered into his*
[the persecutor's] *hand until a time and* [two] *times and half*
a time. (Dan. vii. 25.)

—that is to say, for three and a half "times" (years) in all.
This strange expression is deliberately chosen, it would
seem, to throw sinister light upon an historical fact. The
Syrian persecution lasted from June, 168 to December of
165 B.C. This symbolic figure associated here with the idea
of distress may possibly explain why our Lord should
speak of three and a half years of famine in the time of
Elias whereas the original account seems to suggest a
somewhat shorter period[1]. So: addition and multiplica-
tion for plenitude, subtraction and division for defect.

But the play becomes fast and furious when numbers are
represented by letters of the alphabet, and this is as true of
Hebrew as it is of Greek. The game was early in vogue.

[1] cf. Luke iv. 25 and Jas. v. 17 with 3 Kings xviii. 1.

Writing at some time between A.D. 80 and 130, the author of the uninspired *Epistle of Barnabas* argues that Abraham foresaw the Crucifixion. He deduces it from the number of Abraham's servants—318. The Greek letter *tau*, he points out, has 300 for its numerical value and it is written in the form of a cross (T). This leaves 18 unaccounted for but the author is not baffled. The first two letters of the holy name will supply that; *I*'s equivalent is ten and *E*'s is eight!

St. John himself does not disdain the game. He warns us that he is playing it, though very seriously, when he writes:

Here is wisdom! Let intelligent ones work out the Beast's number which is [actually] *a Man's number. And his number is 666.* (Apoc. xiii. 18.)

Without stirring the attention of the Roman authority John could thus warn the Christians that Nero, the great persecutor, still lived in the person of his successors—that this devouring Beast still hungered for the Church. In Hebrew letter-figures, unknown of course to the Romans, Caesar Nero (*qsr nrwn*) produces the sum of 666. This number was suitable from other points of view also. It fell pointedly short of the symmetrical and perfect 777. It was, too, the very contrast of the supra-perfect 888 which is the sum of the Greek letters of the name of Jesus (IESOUS: 10,8,200,70,400,200). Indeed the Beast was a thrice-sinister thing; the very antithesis and antagonist of Christ.

Now cabbalism as an author's trick is one thing but cabbalism as a common principle of interpretation is quite another. That the Apocalypse of John should have been, as it still is, the victim of this last is not surprising— apocalypses deliberately invite this sort of thing, though the instrument of interpretation is lethal in irresponsible hands. But cabbalism off its own stamping-ground is a rogue-elephant. An example:

Saul was a child of one year when he began to reign and he reigned two years over Israel. (1 Kings xiii. 1.)

And yet he already stood head and shoulders above the tallest of his subjects! (1 Kings x. 23). The Douay foot-note is artless: "That is, he was good and like an innocent child and for two years continued in that innocency". But perhaps this is not such a bad commentary on the text *as we have it.* Look now:

As almost all critics are agreed, the text is corrupt. From the little evidence we have it appears that Saul was thirty years of age when he became king; he ruled for forty. Now it is not the term "child" that worries us: the semitic phrase "child of", in this connection, means simply "aged"; thus Isboseth is called "a child of forty years" elsewhere in the books of Kings.[1] No, the corruption has occurred in the numbers and it seems probable that for "one" and "two" the original text read "thirty" and "forty". But corruption of manuscripts cannot be idly supposed. If evidence is lacking from other texts or versions we must be able to assign some reasonable cause either for error or for deliberate change. Now the letters that stand for "one" and "two" are not easily confused, in any form of the Hebrew alphabet, with the letters that represent "thirty" and "forty". Mere error, then, appears to be an insufficient explanation.

The answer lies, not improbably, in the intrusion of a cabbalistic marginal note. The cabbalist was rampant already in the first centuries of the Christian era and to extract hidden meanings he had recourse to various shifts. The pertinent instance is the rule called *"Albam"* (mnemonic word for: A—L; B=M) by which the Hebrew alphabet was bisected and the letters of the second half substituted for the corresponding letters of the first half.

[1] 2 Sam. ii. 10, Hebrew text; cf. Douay Version 2 Kings ii. 10.

Or, of course, vice-versa. Thus in the Hebrew alphabet A answers to L, B to M, C (G) to N and so on. Now since L stands numerically for 30 and M for 40, the *"Albam"* substitution would give respectively 1 (A) and 2 (B). Now this *may* be pure coincidence but it is rather too striking to be ignored.

Yet to what purpose the substitution, if substitution there was? What was the hidden meaning extracted, or rather intruded? We can only guess. Nevertheless it is certain that the early Jewish commentators, who were followed by the Christian Fathers, explain the text exactly as the Douay note explains it. And they stand every chance of understanding the mentality of their compatriots and near-contemporaries. It is therefore conjectured that the Rabbis had used this cabbalistic device to justify God's choice of Saul and his subsequent rejection. Hidden in the text, they suggested, was the reason for this contradiction—the original innocence and later unfaithfulness of the king. This they indicated in a marginal note (reading "A" and "B") which later crept into the text itself.[1]

Caution, therefore. Should an author deliberately underline his numerals, as Matthew does in his first chapter, or should the whole tone of his book be fantastical, as in the case of apocalyptic writing, we may accept the implicit invitation to scrutinize the figures. Otherwise we should tend to be sceptical in this matter. Broadly speaking, the more obvious the schematism of the number and the further removed from concrete probabilities, the more chance there is of symbolism. On the other hand, symbolism does not necessarily preclude concrete reality—it may presuppose it and build upon it. But still, we should be shy of symbolism when the more obvious meaning suffices.

It is forty years now since Loisy suggested that John's

[1] Cf. *Biblica*, 1926, 193-203. By the way, the first letter of the Hebrew alphabet, here called "A", is really no more than a consonantal sigh.

"pond, having five porches" (John v. 2) symbolized Judaism with its five books of the Law. Unlike Augustine, who had been before him with this interpretation, Loisy held that the symbolism excluded the reality. For justification he alleged the improbability of a pentagonal building. Since then, however, the White Fathers who excavated the place have discovered the five colonnades— not disposed in pentagonal form but as four sides of a rectangle *plus* one that straddles the pool. This sort of thing brings us down to earth.[1]

Consequently, when we meet John's one hundred and fifty-three fish we may still be old-fashioned enough to believe that John had counted them.[2] The historical narrative as a whole has, no doubt, its further symbolical value: that so many and so big fish should have found their way into Peter's net may be symbolic of Peter's success in "catching men". But the number 153? On the desk before me lies open a commentary on St. John's Gospel. Unexpectedly enough it displays a half-page equilateral triangle compound of dots—seventeen at the base and diminishing by units to the apex. Its purpose is to show that 153 is a "triangular number", the sum of the first seventeen natural numbers. This may be interesting but I doubt if it be significant. After all, 136 is a triangular number like 171 and so forth. We may be forgiven, too, for thinking John more of a Galilean fisherman and less of a Greek mathematician. When the commentator assures me that John thus depicts "a perfect and unique catch of fish" I am tempted to remind him, with respect, of the mountain and the laughable mouse. He himself would be justly irritated were I to accuse him of hidden meaning when he treats, as he does, of the number 153 on page 553. There is such a thing as coincidence.

[1] Cf. *Revue Biblique*, 1937, p. 329.   [2] John xxi. 11.

XIV

AND GOD SAID TO MOSES . . .

When we talk to babies we lisp as they do.

(St. John Chrysostom.)

Israel was a child and I loved him. (Osee ii. 1.)

IN THESE days of slippery argument when it is as easy to
impale an adversary as to fork an oyster we have come to
love a great thumping howler.

It is many years now since I dipped into Mr. Aldous
Huxley's "End and Means" but I remember how, among
other pleasantries, he compared our rosaries to praying-
wheels. Well, why not? Had he chosen to liken them to
the pebbles in an umpire's pocket we should still not complain. But if he thus implies that we are beseeching
Buddha or counting the balls in an over? Ah, then we
beg leave to put him right. And the game of Comparative
Postures goes on—confused too often, alas, with that of
Comparative Religions. Mr. Huxley tells me, with some
solemnity, that when I walk round saying my Breviary I
am in reality performing a ritual dance. Now at this I
laugh—not rudely but heartily withal and in a Christian
spirit. This gifted writer will not, I hope, be offended; he
will remember that where we laugh we love and that true
humility tells us that it is better to be loved than to be
admired. Why do I laugh? Because this is a howler and I
know it. Having performed the gyration over five thousand
times to Mr. Huxley's not-at-all-after which, I think,
we may presume, it would be false modesty to allow that

he knows my intention better than I. Not that I object
to ritual dances—far from it—but one must decline
the compliment here. The intention is more prosaic:
digestion.

But however ill-chosen the example we are not at logger-
heads with the suggestion. We seek only to warn against
hasty conclusions. It is not bad form, I hope, to confront a
twentieth century savant with a scholar of the third.
Now Origen once remarked, in a context we shall explore,
that it is the intention that makes the external act what it
is. He bids us be wary with our esteem. Thus, says he,
adultery may be avoided for many motives. The Stoics
declined it in the interests of personal perfection without
reference to a personal and transcendental Judge and
Father. The Epicureans saw in it an enemy of true personal satisfaction. Most people, Origen cynically goes on,
steer clear of it for fear of the police. Who would say that
such uniform abstinence is not of varying worth? The
intention colours the whole act. Thus in matters ceremonial our alb, for instance, may recall the Roman toga
but we offer no sacrifice to Jupiter Capitolinus. I worship
no Dagon fish-god because I refuse fish except on Friday.
The truth surely is that the great family of man is confined
to certain postures or modes of self-expression. From this
fund each must draw whether it is to pay idols or to pay
God.

Hammurabi's seven-foot column with its three hundred
inscribed laws was unearthed at the beginning of the
century. There was some excitement. Small wonder
since its provisions resembled, in so many cases, those laid
down by Moses about seven hundred years later. It was a
shock to those who had laughed, with Voltaire, at the idea
of Moses being able to write at all in those distant days or
at the quaint story of the stone tablets of the Decalogue.
But it was a shock also to those who had conceived the

Mosaic Law as a garment "off the peg" and not cut to measure.[1]

Much has happened since the discovery of this Babylonian Code of about 2000 B.C. Tablets have come from the ground—Sumerian, Hittite, Assyrian—almost too fast for their decipherers. The Mosaic legislation, in spirit rigidly monotheistic and severely moral, is still a prodigy of the ancient world but the letter of its code is now seen blending into the background of the common law of western Asia. The result is not in every case, indeed not in any case, disturbing. At times it even sheds a welcome light. Thus the oddly insistent prohibition:

Thou shalt not boil a kid in the milk of its dam,[2]

long haunted the commentators. But in 1928 a farmer's plough struck a buried tombstone in northern Phoenicia. And what a harvest! A whole civilization—the civilization of Ugarit whose modern name is Ras Shamra or Fennel Head —and a literature of the fifteenth century before Christ![3] Now the "Poem of the Gracious Gods" in this Phoenician literature, which reflects Canaanite custom, prescribes just that weird ritual which Moses forbids. The prohibition, meaningless before and perhaps even smelling of superstition, now appears as a sound and direct attack by uncompromising monotheism upon Canaanite idolatrous practice.

While we are still on the food-topic: recent discoveries have something to say on the famous pork-question. It was once thought that the ban on pork was originally an hygienic measure and in a country where there is never

[1] Cf. Lagrange, *Historical Criticism and the Old Testament,* English trans., 905.
[2] Exod. xxiii. 19; repeated in Exod. xxxiv. 26 and Deut. xiv. 21.
[3] Cf. e.g. the interesting and measured article of de Vaux in *Revue Biblique,* 1937, 526-555.

an "r" in the month this would not be surprising. Yet in view of the collection of pig-bones found at the "high-place" (shrine) of Gezer it now seems that here too we have an explicit reaction from idolatrous custom. In any case, hygiene will not explain all the food-laws. After all, Israel's neighbours throve on the illegal camel and I am told that the Syrian Bedawin go in for the ostracized mouse.[1]

But let us rather put the case for the prosecution. I mean the *borrowing* of religious customs from paganism or, in some cases, the persistence of pre-Abrahamitic pagan ancestral rites. Circumcision, for instance. You know, religious custom is intensely conservative and therefore betrays its age by its fashions. Now the instrument of circumcision being of stone, despite the manifest convenience of metal, points us back to an origin before the Bronze Age which, for Canaan, means before 2500 B.C. (There is a similar example of tenacity in Exod. xx. 25 where it is prescribed that no metal tool is to work on the stones of the altar.) There is, moreover, historical evidence that the rite of circumcision was practised in Egypt more than a thousand years before Moses and a few hundred before Abraham was called from his idolatry. When, therefore, "God said to Abraham. . . . All the male kind of you shall be circumcised" he did not reveal a hitherto unknown rite but sanctioned existing custom which existed among pagan people. True, he gave it religious significance within a monotheistic people, but why choose a tainted ceremony at all? It is not difficult to see that circumcision, a rite which in origin seems not to have been an hygienic measure but rather a ceremony initiating adult males into the tribe, could be so divinely used. When the "tribe" was a nation consecrated to the one God the rite of initiation would have a sound, religious

[1] Lev. xi. 4 (camel); Lev. xi. 29 (mouse).

significance. But there remains with us a vague wish that God had chosen some other symbol.

This is but one of many difficulties. If we are to judge by the Council of Jerusalem in A.D. 49, more important even than circumcision was abstention from blood-meat. The Council refused to impose circumcision on the gentiles yet recommended the application of this food-law.[1] This prohibition of blood-meat, still observed in some Christian circles as late as the eighth century, is based on the primitive conviction that the blood holds the life of the animal.[2] This mysterious quality of blood doubtless explains the precautions with which the primitives surrounded its consumption. But how strange that God should permit this superstitious esteem among his own people! Here again, however, we must beware of putting the case against ourselves too strongly. In fact this esteem for blood had lost its superstition by the time it reached the Mosaic Law. Whatever the biological exactitude of the "life in the blood" statement (Lev. xvii.14), with which exactitude the inspired author is not concerned, it is clear that Israel abstained from blood not through fear of lurking spirits but as a symbolic means of acknowledging God as sole lord of life. Nevertheless, the pagan associations of the idea are perhaps disquieting.

To make fully sure that we do not underestimate the difficulty let us take one or two more bizarre examples. It would be quite false to imagine that the Law, much less the Old Testament as a whole, is swarming with these oddities but we wish to make it plain that we are not evading the issue. Take the *Urim* and *Tummim*, now. Considerable doubt attaches both to their names and to their nature but "oracles" and "formulae" perhaps

[1] The word " kosher " applied to this law is from the Hebrew root *ksr* " to be fitting ", hence " meat slain in a way fitting the requirements of the Law ".
[2] Cf. Lev. xvii. 11-14; Deut. xii. 23.

translates them. They appear to have been two stones, or pieces of wood, placed in the burse or *ephod* which hung at the high priest's breast. They were distinguished one from the other by a difference either of colour or of inscription. The yea or nay of the ruler's course of action was determined according to which of the two was drawn out by the priest. This procedure later gave way to the practice of consulting God's prophets, a practice much more intelligible and congenial to our minds. Yet, to our surprise, such casting of lots to learn God's will is still found among the Apostles: in this way Matthias took his place in the apostolic circle (Acts i. 26). Again we are uneasy: it looks suspiciously like imitation of pagan divinatory practice.

And then the strange ritual of the Red Cow in the book of Numbers (xix.1–22). The heifer was sacrificed "outside the camp"[1] and its ashes placed in water to purify those who had touched the dead. It is true that the choice of a cow may be a reaction from the Egyptian veneration for that animal but the ceremony as a whole has its parallels in pagan rituals. Of course, these matters it is the symbolism and not the symbol that counts. For the Hebrews, it appears, the ashes of an animal sacrificed to expiate sin symbolized purification and thus reinforced the natural symbolism of the water in which the ashes were placed. But why should God have tolerated, even "enjoined", an elaborate ceremonial shared by the pagans?

Lastly, the "waters of jealousy". The ritual is described in Numbers v. 11–31. The suspected wife was taken to the Sanctuary; there she was made to drink of water into which was placed soil from the ground of the Tabernacle. In this water the written accusation had been dipped and

---

[1] The "purity" conferred was of course merely legal as was the "offence". The Epistle to the Hebrews compares and contrasts the inward efficacy of the blood of Christ. (Heb. ix. 13ff.)

dissolved. (We might observe, in the passing, that this practice may help to throw light on St. Paul's "eateth and drinketh judgement" threat for those who unworthily take the Holy Eucharist; cf. 1 Cor. xi. 29.) If guilty and obstinately silent the woman would be struck with disease, possibly dropsy. The very publicity of this detailed performance would tend to restrain the husband from light suspicion and the wife from stubborn silence; it would favour trust and private reconciliation. It is not surprising, therefore, that we have no record of any such ceremony having taken place; cases must have been extremely rare. It is significant that the Law ascribes this chastisement to God and not to any magical efficacy of the water but the rite itself suggests similar "trials by ordeal" among the pagan peoples.

Suggestive comparison has been made, too, of the Hebrew monthly feast of the New Moon (*Neomenia*) with the moon-worship of Egypt and Assyria. But that the prophets do not complain of it is ample evidence that it did not savour of idolatry. Moreover, we have a ready answer from Christian practice. From the fourth century our Lord's birthday was saluted on the Roman feast, December 25th., of the "Unconquered Sun" rising again to power after the winter solstice. No doubt this was plain defiance—a gauntlet thrown down by the Light of the World. And yet it is probable, too, that there was something of diplomacy in it: if the Romans *must* have a feast on that date, let it be a proper one! This is not mentioned idly. It is precisely of such diplomacy that we have now to speak.

> If we were to understand such laws literally
> I should blush to confess that God gave them.

So said Origen, speaking of certain curiosities in the Old Law. Accordingly, trained in the exegetical dentistry of

Alexandria, he used the anaesthetic of allegory to extract many painful points. To do him justice, this genius was entirely at one with Justin and others on the principle of "condescension" of which we are about to treat. It was by this principle that he explained the *urim* and *tummim*, for instance. That he did not apply the principle more generally is possibly because he did not realize its full implications; but it is more probable that a lack of known pagan parallels made certain practices appear to him pointless unless they had an allegorical significance. With the knowledge that we have to-day and with the sobriety of the Antiochene school of "proper" literal interpretation we refuse to imitate Origen in this allegorizing mood. The literal sense is all too plainly intended by the legislator. Are we therefore to blush? Are the Mosaic oddities unworthy of a revealing God? Possibly. But who said "revealing"? You will recall that revelation in the narrow sense is not the same thing as Inspiration at all. Come, let us be plain and as brief as may be.

God chooses men, not robots. When he chooses a nation he accepts a living thing with ingrained customs. He does not annihilate centuries of national formation. When he seized the tiller of Israel he did not fit a Diesel engine and throw the sailing-tackle overboard. He steered for harbour with every ragged sail flying in every breeze that blew. "Ah, there you go", says Prodnose, "always a specious answer! New lamps for old!". "New?", say I, "Rubbish!".

If you want a robust view of the Old Law and of its many outlandish practices—and no one will complain that we have not given them fair prominence—go to the early Christian writers. They recognized readily enough that the Hebrew nation, idolatrous in its origins as in its contacts, had marked paganizing tendencies. *To these tendencies they regarded almost all the complicated ritual of the Old*

Law as a concession. There, now. Is that robust or not?
Their cry is "*Sugkatabasis*" which is, in inadequate English,
"Condescension". They had well learned the Gospel
lesson of the fatherliness of God. On this solid and simple
foundation they build its consequences. Our Lord himself
had given a broad hint on this very point:

Moses by reason of the hardness of your hearts permitted *you to
put away your wives but from the beginning it was not so.*
(Matt. xix. 8).

This accounts for Justin's boldness in the second century[1].
He coldly informs the Jew that his dispensation was God's
tolerance, not God's preference; that it was a *second-best*.
God, as Irenaeus was to say a few years later, made himself a baby with man. Like a father he played on the floor
with the children (and we have to use the word "condescension" for this!). But the dolls and golliwogs must bend
their knees in his honour. These toys of Israel—what are
they but Sacrifice, the Temple and, as Tertullian adds,
the food-laws and many other "fussy pettifoggeries"
("negotiosae scrupulositates")? Chrysostom who is the
great exponent of the *Sugkatabasis*[2] even says that God
did not *want* sacrifices:

When he forbade sacrifice to demons he countenanced
sacrifices that he did not really want in order to secure what
he did want.

To those who have toiled through the Pentateuchal
minutiae relative to sacrifice this plain speaking comes as a
relief and a shock. It throws some light on the vigour of
the prophetic language regarding the secondary importance of sacrifice: "I desire mercy", says Osee, "and not

[1] For this and other references see the splendid treatment in Fr. Pinard
de la Boullaye's *L'Étude Comparée des Religions* (Paris, 1929), I, 552-571.
[2] Cf. *Biblica*, 1933, 330-347.

F

sacrifice" (Osee vi. 6). And St. Jerome goes so far as to suggest that the Levitical, tribal, priesthood idea may have been borrowed from paganism.

The "condescension" reached its peak in the Incarnation: the Word spoke with the tongue of man still but the tongue was his own. And the "condescension" will go on as long as man is man and God is Father. Which, after all, brings us back to the praying-wheel business.

We have most deliberately emphasized the likenesses of pagandom and Israel. It is not here within our scope to indicate the depth of the difference. Yet it must be made clear that the likeness sits lightly on the surface. Thus the immoralities of the pagan cults, sacred murder, sacred prostitution and the like, are rigorously banned from Mosaic practice. It is needless to say that the early Christian writers never held, as we do not hold, that God sanctioned pagan religious ceremonies just as they were. But their shrewd assessment of God's economy taught them to see how He could draw upon an existing stock of ritual to coax His people to Himself. What if He had done otherwise? He would have gained either rebels or slaves.

The principle of the second century anticipated the discoveries of the twentieth. We should do well to remember it ourselves when the oddities of the Old Law are lightly mocked. We should recall it, too, when they are heavily urged as they are by orthodox Jewish neighbours. We shall remember that God did not reveal this custom and that; rather He adopted a nation and, with it, its customs *en masse*. We shall remember that this adoption meant nothing if it did not mean the Godward direction of these customs. But direction is not destruction. We shall begin to understand how so much of the Law of the unchanging God may pass when, in time's fullness, mankind itself has learned to put away the things of a child. After the manner of the early Fathers we shall approach with caution such phrases as: "And God said to Moses. . . ". We shall not always see in them a headline heralding divine dictation but perhaps only a toleration of existing custom.

To this robust outlook, if we have lost it, we must return. The Holy Father himself invites us when he recalls to our notice the principle of "condescension" dear to the great Chrysostom.[1]

[1] Encyclical *Divino Afflante*, 1943, CTS. trans. par. 41.

XV

THE NEW TEMPLE

Wisdom hath built herself a house. (Prov. ix. 1.)

THEY TELL me that Michelangelo dissected nearly a score of dead bodies in pursuit of his art: hundreds of minute sketches are evidence. Yet this was but a preparation; the sketches are not found upon the ceiling of the Sistine Chapel. But in truth they are: behind the powerful face of the Father, within the thrust of the flying cherubim lurks all that painstaking scaffolding of anatomy. In them it is not destroyed but fulfilled; the skeletons have achieved round flesh and they live. And it is indeed the law of all life that nothing wholly dies but lends its parting elements to new living. Man and his institutions make no exception to this inexorable plan; hence the impermanence of his own efforts at violent and utter change. And when God plans for man in a special way—we can use only human terms—the continuity of design will be clearer still. Not an iota of the old document nor a flourish of the old sketch but will play its part in the new writ and in the finished design. The perfect work may appear in history as suddenly as the Sermon on the Mount but you may be sure that the Master has been labouring for centuries.

Now not the prophets alone but the whole strange history of God's people carried portfolios of his sketches many years before mankind was to see the radiance of his splendour and the full expression of his being shining through the face of his Son.[1]

[1] Cf. Heb. i. 1-3; 2 Cor. iv. 6.

The Old Testament was a rehearsal, though not a full-dress rehearsal, for the New. We are not speaking of the actuation of formal prophecies. We are speaking of history repeating itself—more gloriously repeating itself and so remarkably repeating itself that the very repetition appears at once deliberate and divine. It is deliberate because the correspondence is too exact to be fortuitous; it is the argument from the key to the lock. It is divine because no human mind could so have grouped the rough, angular, fitless pieces scattered across the old order of things into a great portrait that came to life.

Eye hath not seen nor ear heard . . . what mighty plans God made for His lovers (1 Cor. ii. 9).

When St. Paul uses these words he is not referring immediately and exclusively to the happiness of heaven but to the whole great and "foolish" divine plan running through history to the Cross.

If I may use a homely picture, the régime of the Old Law was a deflated balloon with its painted pattern shrivelled and indecipherable. But filled with the great wind of the Spirit it has assumed in the days of the incarnate Word a perfection of shape and hence a clarity of design of which the inklings of the prophets themselves fell notably short.[1] Come, then, without further delay to one spoke of our argument. For it is a convergent argument: its effect derives from a convergence of maximum probabilities pointing uncompromisingly to one conclusion. Of these many possible lines of approach (the Law, the Sacrifice, the Priesthood, the Kingship and others) we shall choose one because it is the visible centre and rallying-point of the old régime. I mean the Temple. On this side of heaven we must use our knees:

[1] Eph. iii. 5; 1 Pet. i. 10.

" Look, Michael," said the Padre Eterno gazing down on our little globe, " what are those little things swarming up and down all over it? " " Men, " said Michael. " Oh, " said the Padre Eterno, " but here and there are some not doing as the rest but throwing themselves into all manner of attitudes. What is the meaning of that? " " Sire, " cried Michael, " they are worshipping You! " " Oh, they are worshipping *Me*! Well, that is the most sensible thing I have heard of them yet."[1]

Truly man demands material expression even for the things of the spirit. Yet such expression is only a handmaid and she must be kept in her place. In Israel this expression revolved around the "Glory"—the special manifestation of the divine presence between the two figures of cherubim that crowned the Ark. When the Ark was captured in battle Phinees' wife called her child *I-Kabod* ("Alas, the Glory!") because the Glory had departed from Israel. But the Ark returned and the Glory returned and it filled the stone Temple of Solomon. Yet not for ever. The great destruction of 586 saw the end of Ark and Temple, and Ezechiel it was who now mourned the departure of the Glory from Temple and City:

And the Glory of Yahweh rose above the centre of the city and paused upon the hill that lies to the east of the city. (Ezech. xi. 23.)

In the prophet's vision the departing Glory rests for a moment upon Olivet. Strangely enough it was upon this very hill that our Lord sat and pronounced the desolation of the Temple of his own time— the abomination of desolation standing in the Holy Place; the final departure of the Glory. He almost invites us to see that he himself is the Glory driven out by the obstinacy of his own Sion

[1] From Belloc's *Path to Rome*.

*Jerusalem, Jerusalem, how often would I have gathered. . . !
And thou wouldst not. Behold your house [temple?] shall be left
to you desolate because, I say, you shall not see me henceforth . . . .*
(Matt. xxiii. 37–39.)

But meanwhile the hand of history had not been idle.
Providence was roughly chiselling away the stone that
threatened to encase the heart. It was a painful operation
but a necessary one if the heart was to survive. Jeremias
foresaw it ten years before its coming. He appreciated its
urgency: superstitious attachment to external forms
menaced the substance of religion itself. He protested
loudly:

*Trust not to empty words crying: The Temple of God, the
Temple of God, the Temple of God.* (Jer. vii. 4.)

No wonder Jeremias was unpopular. His perspective was
too exact for his time and his boldness unbearable:

*No longer shall you have the Ark of the Lord's Covenant for your
rallying-cry. From thought and memory it will have passed away.*
(Jer. iii. 16. Knox Version.)

Alarming and, thought his fellows, alarmist hints that a
stone Temple might pass. What could Israel be without
the Glory, without the Presence? But perhaps one or two
thoughtfully asked themselves if the Stone and the Glory
must always go together.

Even when the Temple of Solomon lay in ruins the
exiles in Babylon were taught to expect the return of the
Glory. Ezechiel was their teacher. He promised a Temple
to which the Glory would return but his language is so
remarkable and so strongly dosed with allegory that the
exiles must have suspected, as we are sure, that such a
Temple could never be made with human hands. His last
nine chapters are full of it and the last two in particular

suggest symbolism by their very geographical extravagance. To this strange, if not wholly ideal, Temple the Glory will return:

And the Glory (kabod) *of Yahweh went into the Temple by way of the eastern gate.* (Ezech. xliii. 4.)

For these same exiles the second part of the prophecy of Isaias has a like message of consolation, a message which the Gospels will later make their own. Across the desert that divides Babylon from Palestine the Glory will go home again:

In the desert prepare ye the way of the Lord . . . Let every valley be filled . . . Then the Glory of Yahweh shall be revealed and all flesh together shall see it. (Isa. xl. 3f.)

And yet when the exiles did return after seventy years (in 537) the Temple they contrive to build was only a poor shadow of Solomon's so that the elders wept to see it. And the Glory was absent, too, as the Rabbis insist[1]. For Zacharias and, after him, Malachy, the Glory was yet to come:

And presently Yahweh . . . shall come to His Temple. (Mal. iii. 1.)

Four hundred disappointing years slipped away before a voice in Israel could cry in triumph that the promises of Isaias and of Malachy were realities at last and Mark opens his Gospel with the words of the two prophets:

Behold I send my angel before thy face who shall prepare the way before thee. A voice of one crying in the desert: Prepare ye the way of the Lord, make straight his paths. (Mark i. 2–3.)

---

[1] Cf. on all this, Hebert, *Authority of the Old Testament,* 1947, especially pp. 148-154. Cf. also the fine article by Dubarle in *Revue Biblique,* 1939, pp. 21-44.

It seems that the Baptist was a second Isaias, herald of the returning Presence and of the Glory tabernacled this time not in canvas nor in stone but in flesh:

And the Word was made flesh and set up his tent among us, and we saw his Glory. (John i.14.)

Now our Lord's first great claim, as it was the last charge against him, lay full in the stream of the course of thought which we may call the Temple-tradition. It was at the very beginning of our Lord's ministry (with great probability) that he uttered the sentence that was to be used for his destruction:

Destroy this temple and in three days I will raise it up. (John ii. 19.)

It is significant that our Lord had just quoted a sentence of Jeremias ("You have made it a den of thieves") which comes from that very passage in which the prophet expressed his misgivings concerning the attachment to a Temple of stone (Jer. vii. 4, 11). Possibly, too, Jesus hints that the old sacrifices may cease since he drives the sacrificial animals from the precincts. In any case it is plain that he, like Jeremias, does not shrink from the prospect of an Israel without its stone Temple. But he refuses to envisage his new Israel without any Temple at all. With Ezechiel and Malachy (iii. 1–4) he thinks of a greater and a purer Temple still. We have the evangelist's word for it:

He spoke of the temple of his body.

Two or three years later at the Trial the witnesses declared, rightly or wrongly, that his actual words had been: ". . . . I will build another not made with hands"

F*

(Mark xiv. 58). They were thinking, no doubt, of a stone Temple miraculously erected but in effect he had spoken of a Temple of flesh "not made with hands, not of this creation".[1] For the old shrine he would offer in exchange his own glorified Body—a Temple in which "dwelleth the fullness of the Godhead". Small wonder that he could say of himself, surrounded by his little group of disciples: "I tell you that there is here a greater thing than the Temple".[2] Now whatever the witnesses at the Trial thought, it is clear that the high priest saw in the objectionable words more than a boast of prodigious power. He sensed the enormity of our Lord's claim: the Accused contemplated with calm the passing of the old régime but he went further—he counted himself competent to supplant it in his own messianic person. Such a pretention was monstrous in the high priest's ears and explains his question shot out seemingly without logical connection: "Art thou the Son of God?". This title our Lord had used; something of its tremendous implication had at last emerged. To this charge in this context our Lord pleaded guilty and on this charge he was condemned.

During the Easter season we sing the words: *Vidi aquam egredientem de templo a latere dextro*—"I saw waters pouring from the right flank of the temple." They seem an untimely reminder of the sadness of Good Friday with its contemplation of the pierced side of Christ. But the verse we sing is in fact the "new canticle"—the triumphant song of the new order conceived on the Cross in sorrow but born in joy from the garden Tomb. It is the *risen* Body that is the Temple of the new era. John, who stood by the Cross, was very careful to notice that water flowed from his Lord's heart but it is John, too, who warns us that the

[1] Heb. ix. 11. This interpretation is that of Chrysostom and the Greek commentators.
[2] Col. ii. 9; Matt. xii. 6.

great sluices of the Spirit opened only with the Resurrection (John vii. 39). The water from the side of the Crucified is only a symbol and a promise, an assurance issuing from our Lord's own heart.

Whence this connection of water and temple? It would be difficult to trace its deep roots. There is some link, perhaps, with Moses who struck the rock for water. But it is certain that the idea appears fully-grown in Ezechiel and it is from him (xlvii. 2) that our Easter hymn is taken. In the prophets the great Future is seen more often as a Kingdom; here in Ezechiel it appears as a Temple pouring forth a broad and healing stream:

And last, he took me to the door of the temple itself, and shewed me where a stream of water flowed eastwards from beneath the threshold of it. . . . Wherever it flows, he told me, there shall be teeming life. (Ezech. xlvii. 1, 9. Knox Version.)

When Zacharias looks to the future Age he also sees the great healing stream but this time we feel nearer to its source:

I shall pour out upon the house of David a spirit of grace. . . . Whom they have pierced they shall mourn as one mourns an only son. But in the day there shall be a fountain open . . . for the washing of the sinner. (Zach. xii. 10-xiii. 1.)

St. John has just called his readers' attention to the water running from the open side of Christ, he now reminds them of this passage of Zacharias with its rich source of grace:

They shall look on him whom they pierced. (John xix. 37.)

It is the same John who, steeped in Ezechiel's vision, sees the new order, which he calls "the new Jerusalem", as a great temple with its water of life:

Behold the tabernacle of God with men. . . .   To him that thirsteth I will give of the fountain of the water of life. . . .   The Lord God is the temple thereof and the Lamb. (Apoc. xxi–xxii.)

But it was our Lord himself who had given him the ideas. He had spoken of "the Temple of his Body"; he had spoken also of the flowing waters:

Jesus cried out in the temple. . . .   If any man thirst let him, believing in me, come to me and drink.   As the scripture saith [of me] : Forth from his bosom shall flow rivers of living water. . . . Now this he said of the spirit. . . . [1]

Nor is it by accident that, having offered himself as the source of living waters to the Samaritan woman at the well, he should go on to say that the old Temple would be needed no longer:

The water that I will give him shall become in him a fountain of water springing up into life everlasting. . . .   The hour cometh when you shall neither on this mountain nor in Jerusalem adore the Father . . . but . . . in spirit and truth. [2]

Much more might have been said of this synthesis of Old and New. Side by side with the doctrine of the Mystical Body St. Paul places the thought of the Mystical Temple. As the Christian is a member of the Body, so is he a stone in the Temple (Eph. ii. 21f.). But we have attemped to lift only a corner of the veil that hangs over the great preparatory ideas of the Old Testament. In doing so we have not been looking for the obvious resolution of literal prophecy; we do not need, therefore, to meet the objections of those who stubbornly protest that the history of the New Testament was adjusted to make it square with the

[1] John vii. 38-39. This translation represents what appears to be the better punctuation of the verses.

[2] John iv. 14, 21, 23. The Samaritan woman in order to turn the embarrassing question about her " husband " introduces the controversial topic of Samaritan worship on the hill adjacent to the well (Garizim).

ancient promises. Nor have we seen merely a cunning assemblage of scattered prophetic pieces of mosaic. This might possibly have been achieved, though with difficulty, by some human genius. We have seen a living and dynamic idea coming to unimaginable maturity not by way of an artful theological thesis but as it were casually and in widely-spread texts. It is not man's work. The prophets themselves only throw out the hints, and had some human, Christian, mind attempted this massive synthesis we should be admiring the great tapestry and not assembling the threads. But, in any case, was any human mind capable of this conception of the Returned Presence and the Temple of Flesh? Rather it is the mind of One alone who could assimilate into himself the raw matter of the prophets and build it up into his own living person.

XVI

OURSELVES AND ISRAEL

O father Abram, what these Christians are
Whose own hard dealings teaches them suspect
The thoughts of others!

(The Merchant of Venice.)

JUDAISM to-day does not speak with one voice. It is not easy, therefore, for the Christian to define his own attitude towards his Jewish neighbour. And yet he must seek to do so:

Hath God cast away his people? God forbid! (Rom. xi. 1.)

and if God has not, how dare we? By what authority may we wash our hands of the Jews? After all, the good old jokes are fairly stale now and the good old hate, the more sinister for seeming pious, was always of the devil. And the coldest thing of all—how it must have seared!—was the old contempt:

His name was Hash Baz Ben and Jedadiah too
And Solomon and Zabulon, this bus-directing Jew.

Oh, I am not trying to whitewash the Race. I believe, and shall attempt to show, that it is the more or less responsible victim of a dark disease of the inner eye. But if the cataract is operable, as with God's grace it is, then it is our business to locate it and, if possible, remove it. We judge of no *individual's* worth in God's sight, whether Gentile's or

Jew's. We consider a *community*—and in trembling humility because Paul warns us: "[God's] graciousness is for thee only so long as thou dost continue in his grace; if not, thou too shalt be pruned away. Just so they too [the Jews] will be grafted in, if they do not continue in their unbelief." (Rom. xi. 22f.) If there is any chance of our understanding each other it is surely here. Now you have been warned that there are many voices in Israel but, on occasions, they harmonize.

In 1933, a small company of Jewish lawyers came together in Rome to re-examine the case against our Lord. They published their verdict of acquittal; it was a gesture to that Holy Year which was being celebrated in Christendom as the nineteenth anniversary of the Crucifixion. A blasphemous impertinence? It was not meant so. In any case it is a symptom; it is matter for cautious hope. If Israel is ever to know and love her Messiah she must first come to appreciate him. To appreciate him? Yes, and to be proud of him. And there are signs of this, too. Recent Jewish literature is eager to remind us that our Lord came from Israel and lived for Israel.[1] It is anxious to prove that all but the smallest clique were guiltless of the blood of Christ. We do not accept without reserve the present attempts to rehabilitate the Pharisees. Nor can we accept the suggestion, gratuitous and flouting the evidence, that the evangelists have thrust themselves between us and the historical facts, unscrupulously throwing all the blame upon Israel. But we do accept these tentative steps towards our Lord and we thank God for them.

There is no solution to the "Jewish Problem" other than the total elimination of Judaism. This is not a ferocious statement. I do not recommend the liquidation of the fifteen million members of the race. Had we no principles of our own we should still shiver to find ourselves thinking

[1] Cf. *Jésus et Israel*, by Jules Isaac, Paris, 1948.

with the Hitlers of the world. It does indeed give us pause
when we find the one philosophy striking at Jew and
Christian with the one rod: perhaps we have something in
common? No, I mean that there is no solution on the
human plane. Does this need proof? Has not everything
been tried and failed? When I speak of eliminating Judaism,
I mean Judaism and not the Jews. Our problem is identical
with the Baptist's. We must seek the "repentance"
of Judaism or better, and closer to the Greek term used by
the Gospels in this connection[1], the change of its whole
moral outlook, the "turning" the prophets are always
pleading for and which we call by its Latin name "conversion". But how can we change this outlook unless we
understand what it is? What *is* wrong with Israel?

A year or so ago a Jew wrote that Christianity has made
three fatal mistakes none of which was inherited from
Judaism. This fatal trinity? "Love your enemies"; "Lay
not up treasures on earth"; "Resist not evil". These three
dreams, the author protests, have held Christianity in a
stupor, powerless to help a world groaning for justice.
Judaism, he goes on, has never fallen into this trap, has
never renounced the prosperity of this world. Judaism
therefore is abreast of the social problem. Judaism is
up-to-date.[2]

A cunning thrust, to be sure. But it is not my business
here to argue that charity may prove in the end a stronger
thing than justice, nor to question whether happiness does
lie in wealth after all, nor to remind our Jewish friend that
the Sermon on the Mount legislated not for governments
but for individual souls. I wish simply to diagnose the
sickness of Judaism and, it would appear, here we have
found a symptom. It must be conceded that Christianity
is not pre-eminently administrative; it hungers first for

[1] Cf. Joüon, *L'Évangile de Jésus-Christ*, Paris, 1930.
[2] M. Braunschvig, *Le vrai visage d'Israël. De Jésus a Hitler*, 1948.

personal justness[1] which is a love of God overflowing to neighbour. It has no great organized plan for the allotment of charity—unless we can call that a plan which fills the nursing ranks with nuns and not with civil servants. The outlook of Judaism, on the other hand, is at once more practical and more material. No one would deny its sons their high and shrewd assessment of the earth's goods. That this gift belongs to them all, though we must not forget the lustre they have lent to the arts and sciences, is surely evidence that it is rooted deep in the race itself. The *national* outlook, if we may say this with charity, is biased towards the material.

Does this give us any clue to our profound religious disagreement? A disagreement which dates back by two thousand years? Does it explain why I find in the synagogue the Old Testament only but in the Church the New, and especially the New? It does. It is precisely because the New refused to interpret the Old in a material sense that the New is for the Jew unacceptable. The Christian holds that the Messianic Age is with us; the Jew, tenacious despite incredible delay, believes it still to come. In the prodigious permanence of his own race he sees a guarantee of future glory—and in this we agree with him though we dispute the nature of the glory. The Jew complains that the enormous Fortune of the prophetic message has not yet been offered; the Christian tells him that it has slipped through his fingers. Why is this when the facts are before us all? Because this people which has borne the cross so long cannot see Fortune in the Cross until the incarnate God breaks through to it with his secret: Take up your cross *and follow me*! Driven and driven from the world's house the Jew steals back thinking he has left his treasure there. Perhaps when he has forced an entry he will find

[1]Cf. Matt. v. 6, where for "justice" read "justness", "holiness" (Westminster and Knox Versions).

the emptiness and his heart may open to the riches of Christ.

But meanwhile this most intelligent race cannot understand that its true fortune may be of the spirit—and the greater for that. It was always so. Stephen stigmatized it for ever as "resistance to the holy spirit" (Acts vii. 51). *To Abraham were the promises made and to his seed*—yes, but Judaism has never been convinced that the Spirit could raise up children to Abraham from the very stones, nor that the promises were to be as spiritual in character as its heirs were to be spiritual in origin. For Judaism this is all a great disappointment, a miscarriage of the promises; for the Christian it is the transcendental fulfilment, the only climax worthy of Israel's God who is a Spirit. And certainly Israel should have expected a climax of some sort. Her own prophets had played upon the recurring rhythm of sacred history but also upon its quickening tempo. Thus, for Isaias, the return from the Babylonian exile is not only another Exodus, it is a greater Exodus:

Thus said Yahweh who made a way in the [Red] *sea and a path in the great waters . . . Remember not the former things, neither consider the things of old* [i.e. the marvels of the Exodus]. *Behold I perform a new thing. . . . Yea, I will make a way in the wilderness, paths in the barren desert.* (Isa. xliii. 16–19. trans. Kissane.)

The men of the New Testament take up the theme. They hail the new era with the words Isaias had used of the return from Babylon:

Prepare ye the way of the Lord; make straight his paths![1]

They know how sad men will think their story but they are not themselves dismayed. When they hail the new

[1] Luke iii. 4ff; cf. Isa. xl. 3ff.

era which is an age not of human prosperity but of the abounding Spirit, they are not ashamed to recall the old promises. They seem calmly confident that their good news is the climax of the repetitive historical crescendo which is the authentic message of the prophets. And those who have learned to assess true religious values cannot disagree. That a nation of God was born from the Egyptian travail was not a small thing; that its remnant returned from Babylon to become a religious community was a greater; that there should be offered deliverance from the dark Overlord of all paganism was surely the greatest. Israel, Judaism, Christianity—this is the ascending sequence, not unexpected and entirely providential. The New Testament is the third great blast upon the triumphant horn of deliverance—but the breath is of the Spirit and the note is too high, alas, for the ear of Israel.

It is puzzling and disappointing that it should be so because the Israel of our Lord's time did in fact await a climax of its own history. The manna would come again and water from the rock; Elias would return, and David, and Sacrifice, and the Temple. And all more glorious. One is almost tempted to add: "and in spiritual form" because the "manna", for instance, was to be fashioned in the third heaven as the Rabbis taught. If it were not a stubborn and unhappy fact it would be incredible that a Jew can refuse the Christian message. Has it not everything to offer him? The Bread that came down from Heaven, the Spring of water leaping to eternal life, a David ruling in lands his father never knew, a Scapegoat to bear the sins of all the world, a Sacrifice to expiate them once and for all? But for the Jew this is all too abstract, too spiritual. What is our task, then—we cannot confer the Spirit? We cannot; that is why, I repeat, there is no solution on the human level. Yet we can pray and we can give good example and (last and least) we can use a little understanding argument. The politician will smile at the solution. Let him. But first let him devise an alternative. Until Israel's Star comes to rest over a mean manger there is no hope. Until Juda's sceptre is a cheap wooden cross there is no hope. This simplicity is of the Spirit.

But there *is* hope and we see great signs. Is it for nothing that the Jewish soul at its best is beginning to be proud of Jesus? I do not believe that this is all cunning, conciliatory policy. Will Israel end by seeing its Christ, even pinned to a cross, as "the glory of Thy people"? Because our own Lord is indeed of that race according to the flesh—and they may come to be of his, according to the spirit. Léon Bloy called Jew-baiting "blasphemy"; it is certainly a hideous perversion to stab Christian charity under the cloak of Christian piety.

Anti-Semitism . . . is the most horrible slap in the face suffered in the continuing Passion of our Lord: it is the most stinging and the most unpardonable because he suffers it on his mother's face and at the hands of Christians.[1]

We say there is hope; we should rather say there is certainty, but it will come in God's good time which may be hastened with our prayers. St. Paul is our guarantee.

The earlier chapters of Paul's Epistle to the Romans are haunted by the fear that Judaism's doctrine of justification by the Law should contaminate his children:

You are not under the Law but under grace . . . you are become dead to the Law by the body of Christ. (Rom. vi. 14; vii. 4.)

And so, throughout those chapters, he pursues the Jewish error as implacably as once he had pursued the Christians.

[1] Léon Bloy, *Le Vieux de la Montagne*; quoted by Maritain in *Redeeming the Time*, London, 1944.

Yet still his heart is torn for his blood-brothers. Listen to the fierce pride in his God-chosen race as he drums out one by one its tremendous privileges until he strikes the great final blow:

. . . my brothers, my kinsmen; Israelites to whom belong the Adoption, the glory, the Covenant, the Law, the Worship, the Promises, the Patriarchs, and of whom (according to the flesh) is Christ, head of all, God for ever blessed. (Rom. ix. 3-5.)

But in the eleventh chapter he turns his mind from the great past and the doubtful present to the glorious and certain future. He surveys the divine plan that stretches over the vast field of all history. He sees that the Gentiles have stormed the breach of the Kingdom over the inert bodies of those who should have led the way. But he sees also these same bodies rising to stare at the happiness within the City and, in the end, to hasten there, moved by a sacred envy:

Blindness has fallen upon a part of Israel but only until the tale of the Gentile nations is complete; then the whole of Israel will find salvation. (Rom. xi. 25. Knox Version.)

Paul's Master had said that the day would come when his blind people would greet him with the Messianic salute: "Blessed is he that cometh in the name of the Lord".[1] When? We cannot know. One thing we do know—that the "nations" must first have their chance. They may have had it already. Another thing we know—that the Jews must first be roused to envy by our appreciation of the Gift, by our example. Have they had that yet? We must each examine his conscience.

Meanwhile two prodigies stand on earth. The Gospel has passed to the four corners of the world and in that

[1] Matt. xxiii. 39; cf. Ps. cxvii. 26.

world, living apart in some dreadful solitude of the spirit, is the strange homogeneous mass of Judaism. Sooner or later these two will meet. Until they do, we shall repeat uncompromisingly with Peter: "The Author of Life you killed, whom God hath raised from the dead". But with all Peter's charity and understanding we shall add: "Brethren, I know that you did it through ignorance".[1] Peter's Master had murmured from the Cross: "Father, forgive them, for they know not what they do". They were mocking him even as he said it. If we have suffered from the same hands let us try to remember that Christ-like charity is a hard and beautiful thing.

[1] Acts iii. 15, 17.

XVII

THE TIP OF THE EAR

As if a shepherd should get out of the lion's mouth two legs or the tip of the ear, so shall the children of Israel be taken out. . . .
(Amos iii. 12.)

TEN years ago died the great Jewish philosopher, Henri Bergson. In his last Will he wrote: "My reflections have led me closer and closer to Catholicism in which I see the complete fulfilment of Judaism." At his own request and with the permission of the Cardinal Archbishop of Paris a priest said prayers at his funeral. Yet he died a Jew. Foreseeing the bitter days of Jewish persecution that lay ahead he could not bring himself to desert his people. It is not for us to rush into judgment upon a noble soul carefully weighing its duty. Better leave that to God. Now Bergson was not the first, nor will he be the last, to be thus troubled:

I am telling the truth in Christ's name . . . when I tell you of the great sorrow, the continual anguish I feel in my heart, and how it has ever been my wish that I myself might be doomed to separation from Christ if that would benefit my brethren, my own kinsmen by race. (Rom. ix. 1–3. Knox Version.)

This language of Paul's is not of logic nor of theology but it is the voice of a profound sentiment. If we would ever understand the strong family bond of Judaism we should read and re-read it. If Christian universalism forbids us to renounce the Jewish case as hopeless, it bids us learn to sympathize with it; and where there is no understanding there can be no sympathy. We born Catholics find it difficult fully to appreciate even the homesickness of the converted, much less his guilty feeling of treachery to a dear and losing cause. Dante placed the traitors in the cold hell.

What, then, would we have said to Bergson? What are we to say to his brothers? Have we the right to sit back, or even to kneel down, and leave the rest to some efficacious grace—for indeed all will be owed to grace in the end? We have not the right. I am my brother's keeper and, by divine privilege, potentially part of that very grace which is to make him safe. I must therefore meet my Jew upon the human plane. Am I to offer him the terrible alternative: Treachery or Eternal Loss? But who said Treachery?

The vice of treachery is opposed to the virtue of patriotism. Now patriotism is not nationalism, nor is nationalism an excess of patriotism any more than superstition is an excess of religion. Nationalism is bad enough wherever we find it but let it grow in the flesh of religion and it will eat and eat like a cancer. This has happened to Israel. To be just, she is not entirely to blame. The prodigious solidarity of the Race, its iron curtain which forbids exit and discourages approach, has been hardened by the hammer of persecution. But this is not all. This almost positive and aggressive exclusiveness has ancient and strong roots: Israel was a chosen *nation*. It is difficult for us to recapture this idea now that we are familiar with the notion of our individual relationship with God and of our individual responsibility before Him. The Israel of old did not start from here. City life has broken down the bond of blood and given us instead the clanship of craft or of class but in Israel's days of quasi-nomadism it was the brotherhood of the tribe that was unshakable. It was individual for group and group against group. Hence the law of vendetta; hence also the primitive justice, of increasing vogue in modern war, in which the foe was a nation and not a guilty clique—a bloodstained, collective entity to be annihilated totally, without distinction.

When God chose this nation he did indeed accept its limitations but he also dedicated himself to its education. Now the direction of this work was precisely towards the idea of the personal and single responsibility of the individual. The beginnings of this movement may be seen in the Law itself but it is the prophets who give it full voice. With them the emphasis shifts from nation to person:

I will make a new covenant . . . not according to the covenant I made with their fathers . . . I will write it in their heart. (Jer. xxxi. 31-33.)

And against the discontented, self-righteous Jerusalemites complaining of their misfortunes, blaming their fathers:

> *The fathers have eaten sour grapes*
> *And the teeth of the children are set on edge,*

Ezechiel firmly placed the blame upon the individual. "The soul", said he, "that sinneth the same shall die" (Ezech. xviii). The national disasters of invasion, deportation, exile should have driven this lesson home. They should have shown Israel that flowers of godliness could flourish in the ruins of their nation; that God could cast aside his old instrument of nationality when he pleased. They should have prepared for a time when there would be neither Jew nor Greek but all one by faith in Christ.

We ask the Jew to shed his nationalism but we beg him to keep his patriotism. We tell him that his race has more to be proud of than it knows. Is it not enough for his just and proper pride that the human nature assumed by the Word himself was a Jewish human nature and that, in the unwitting phrase of the Pharisees, "the whole world is gone after him"? Is it not this, and less than this, which was promised by Zacharias:

In those days ten men of all languages of the Gentiles shall take hold and shall hold fast the skirt of one that is a Jew, saying: 'We will go with you for we have heard that God is with you'? (Zach. viii. 23.)

How, in God's name, can Israel refuse this infinite compliment? How, at least, can the individual and sincere Jew—there are many—resist even this one appeal to prophecy? In all charity I suggest an answer and in all humility I venture a forecast which is the corollary of the answer. The Jew does not think as an individual but, still soaked in the idea of a chosen nation, as a member of a Race. By the destiny of this race he stands or falls— "to Abraham were the promises made and to his seed". What right and what room for independent, personal action when it is to the whole race and to the race as a whole that the prophets offer a glorious future? From this last sentence it follows as a logical and theological conclusion that Israel must move to its future *en masse*. If we cannot prove that sentence false to the satisfaction of the Jew— here is the forecast—we can only hope and pray for a mass conversion which, on human probabilities, would await a dismayingly distant future. But if we *can* prove it false, and we shall now try, then we may help our Jewish friend to see that he may safely, though independent and alone, move from the synagogue into the arms of all the prophets.

It is a commonplace that the prophets foretold a glorious future for Israel. It is also false. It is false, that is, if by

"Israel" we mean what is normally meant: Israel the Nation. Search the prophets—it is woe upon woe for Israel:

"I will shew you what I will do to my vineyard . . . . I will break down the wall thereof and it shall be trodden down and I will make it desolate . . ." The vineyard of the Lord of hosts is the house of Israel. (Isa. v. 5–7.)

For whom, therefore, are the promises? For the Gentiles? Yes, surely:

I said: "Behold Me; behold Me!" to a nation that did not call upon My name. (Isa. lxv. 1.)

But this does not explain the God-given patriotism of the prophets:

Lift up thy voice with strength, thou that bringest good tidings to Jerusalem! Lift it up; fear not! (Isa. xl. 9.)

Nor does it satisfy their conviction that Israel is and shall be in the forefront of God's care:

He that scattered Israel will gather him. (Jer. xxxi. 10.)

We would seem almost to have reached contradiction but, fortunately, the prophets themselves have resolved it for us.

There is a Hebrew word remarkably insistent in the prophetical books. We have no adequate translation for it but the Douay version, happily monotonous, gives us "remnant". It means, as nearly as possible, "the survivors of disaster" considered as a small, compact body. It is just this providential survival of a chosen few that distinguishes Israel's destiny from that of the pagan nations:

Except the Lord of hosts had left us a remnant ["survival"] *we had been as Sodom and we should have been like Gomorrha* [i.e. annihilated]. (Isa. i. 9.)

The word is a reassuring word but it is sinister too: it holds both promise and threat—threat that there should be so few.[1] And these few grow fewer as the prophetic revelation advances. God's message is not born of historical events but it speaks their language: its expression grows with the times. So it is that the idea of the "remnant", the "survivors of disaster", grows clearer-—and, alas, more restricted—as Israel's disasters succeed each other. For the prophets of the eighth century—Amos, Isaias, Micheas—the impending calamity is the Assyrian invasion. As a preacher of to·day would remind us of the narrowness of the gate which leads to Life, so they use the notion of the "remnant" to back their moral appeal. It is already evident that the personnel of this select few is determined, in general, not by God's caprice but by man's behaviour. Man *qualifies* for membership. It is well to remember this for the sake of what follows. Meanwhile let us observe that, for these prophets, the "remnant" is confined to those who are to be spared exile or death at the hand of Assyria. Is this all Israel? Far from it. A mere fraction. The Assyrian deportations from the northern kingdom have left us now with the expression: "the ten lost tribes". Only Juda, and almost negligible Benjamin, remain to inherit the divine promises. Little more than one hundred years later Juda itself has been wasted by the Babylonian and its exiles mourn in captivity but for Jeremias they are the "good figs" of his visionary baskets (Jer. xxiv) and Ezechiel consoles them with the thought that they are the privileged remnant, far from the ruined Temple but with God in their midst and destined to return one day:

[1] On this and the following remarks cf. *Revue Biblique,* 1933, 526-539.

"Alas, O Lord God, wilt thou make an end of all the remnant of Israel?" And the word of the Lord came to me saying . . . "Because I have removed them far off among the Gentiles . . . and have been to them a sanctuary, as it were, in the countries whither they are come. . . . Tell them this: 'Thus saith the Lord God: I will gather you . . . and I will give you the land of Israel'." (Ezech. xi. 13–17.)

But the finances of Babylon, in which many of the exiles shrewdly dabbled, pulled strongly and only a proportion of the exiles returned to the poverty-stricken land of Juda. Reduced by Assyria, reduced by Babylon, reduced by fear for their own comfort, how pitiful is the remnant now! Yet they are the "remnant" and Esdras uses the term when he prays for them (1 Esd. ix. 8) while Zacharias calls this "remnant" (viii. 11) the people of God (xiii. 9). This now is the community which is "Judaism"—the remnant which was heir to the promises and of which was born the Messiah himself. Is it to be diminished still further before the promise comes to fulfilment? Is it to be reduced to one single individual—to the one great Representative of the Jewish people? The thought would lend weight to Paul's strange argument:

To Abraham were the promises made and to his seed. He saith not: And to his seed, as of many; but as of one: And to thy seed which is Christ. (Gal. iii. 16.)

Nevertheless, though this last suggestion may be of interest, it certainly does not exhaust Paul's mind on the subject:

At this present time also there is a remnant saved according to the election of grace. (Rom. xi. 5.)

And what is the qualification now for membership of the remnant? Faith in Christ, the incarnate fulfilment of the promise (Rom. x. 1–21), as of old it had been trust in God who made the promise. Paul laments that, of Israel, only the "elect" ("chosen remnant" Knox Version) have qualified, the rest have been blinded (Rom. xi. 7). To what a few has this remnant shrunk! We think of the three thousand Jews converted on Pentecost Day—a stream quickly dying to a trickle and all but dry in our own times. How many were called and how few chosen![1]

Yet, however dismal this story be we must feel—and our Jewish friend may feel—that this is the natural progress of a great but terrible tragedy; that history and Paul have written with the pen of the prophets. When, therefore, we ask our Jew to take his step alone we ask him only to re-join all that is most holy in the traditions of his race. We assure him that his own prophets foreswore the many to embrace the few. We remind him of the wrench when the courageous few left the majority behind in comfortable Babylon—a painful severance with a great reward. Who then were the traitors? Certainly not the few who tore themselves away. What magic is there in majorities? Nothing but surface-tension. Would Ezechiel have said: Follow the Crowd?

I will judge every one of you according to his ways, O house of Israel. (Ezech. xxxiii. 20.)

There is no treachery but to God.

[1] i.e. "elect" (eklektoi). It is probable that it was to save the lives of these few of Israel that the siege of Jerusalem in A.D. 70 was shortened: "for the sake of the elect those days shall be shortened".